Colin Tribe

Discovering Fingerstyle Ukulele

*An introduction to the technique
of fingerstyle ukulele playing*

ED 13873

Online-Material available – Download all Audio tracks at
en.schott-music.com/fingerstyle-ukulele

www.schott-music.com

Mainz · London · Berlin · Madrid · New York · Paris · Prague · Tokyo · Toronto
© 2018 Schott Music Ltd., London · Printed in Germany

Acknowledgements

I must thank, firstly, my family for their unfailing support during the writing of this book. I started playing the Ukulele when my late wife Maryjka was alive and she would have supported this venture wholeheartedly had she survived to see it completed. My son Rob assisted with the recordings and my daughter Tania sang "I Love Music" in the version included here. Also, I must thank my grandchildren, Megan and Edward, who inspired me to write tunes for them. My delightful students, too, have shared in trying-out some of the pieces and arrangements both in workshops and via "Skype" lessons. And finally, many thanks to my friend Nadia Lasserson, who has been a wonderful and constructive critic throughout and who suggested several of the pieces in the arrangements you will find in this book.

CT

Musical terms

Musical terms are given in the order American (British) at their first mention. American terms are used thereafter.

Note values and other common terms

American		British
whole note	𝅝	semibreve
half note	𝅗𝅥	minim
quarter note	𝅘𝅥	crotchet
eighth note (8ths)	𝅘𝅥𝅮	quaver
sixteenth note (16ths)	𝅘𝅥𝅯	semiquaver
measure		bar
tone		note
whole tone		tone
half step		semitone
staff		stave

Downloading Audio Tracks:

You can download all audio tracks at:
en.schott-music.com/fingerstyle-ukulele

ED 13873
British Library Cataloguing-in Publication Data.
A catalogue record for this book is available from the British Library.
ISMN 979-0-2201-3765-5
ISBN 978-1-84761-479-7

© 2018 Schott Music Ltd, London

Cover design by Adam Hay. Photo: Closeup of ukulele key © Stefan/fotolia.com
Book design by Peter Klein
Photos by Martin Gammon
Ukuleles by LEHO
Printed in Germany

Contents

Introduction

Born to an unlikely parentage of European musical instruments, Portuguese craftsman and the Hawaiian rhythmic spirit, the ukulele came into being around 1890. After arriving in the USA the role of the ukulele as a rhythm chord-playing instrument became firmly established and from the 1920s to the 1950s popular sheet music was published with ukulele chord symbols and diagrams, including practical instructions in retuning the instrument in different keys. By the 1960s guitar chord symbols were almost universally adopted for the ukulele making it easier for players to double on both instruments.

Popular interest in the ukulele has been reignited in the 21st century with many schools and amateur ukulele clubs worldwide having players strumming and singing together for fun, often as an enjoyable social and charitable musical activity. The rhythmic spirit of popular music is being kept alive with the ukulele.

That social and fun arena fed my own introduction to the ukulele which merged quite naturally with my working background as teacher, composer and arranger. It was not long before I began to develop ideas and techniques beyond strumming and to explore the ukulele's capabilities to combine melody, harmony and rhythm all on the one instrument; this is what I call "fingerstyle ukulele", a more open term than "classical ukulele" which is sometimes used.

Inspired by virtuoso players such as Jake Shakimaburko and James Hill, I began arranging (and publishing on *YouTube*) all kinds of music for the instrument; I also devised a ukulele exam syllabus for The Victoria College of Music, London.*)

You don't have to be a virtuoso to enjoy playing more than just chords on the instrument. By following the carefully structured contents of *Discovering Fingerstyle Ukulele*, you can develop the skills that will:

• enable you to play melodies in both the right and left hands with fluidity and expression.

• familiarize you with the chords that all strummers use and help you to discover the many other chord versions to use in your accompaniments. It is not only the right hand that is made to work harder in fingerstyle playing; the left hand, too, will need to gain more strength and flexibility to extend beyond the standard chord patterns. Familiarity with those chords that use all four fingers requires practice, time and patience.

• help you to explore ways to develop rhythmic ideas, sometimes using familiar strums but also to discover the joys of right-hand *p i m a* patterns to create arpeggios and other accompaniment figures.

*) Victoria College of Music, 71 Queen Victoria Street, London EC4V 4AY www.vcmexams.co.uk

Features of *Discovering Fingerstyle Ukulele* include:

• Mixed notation system – Music and TAB

The music is presented in both tablature and standard staff notation. Tablature is a system of lines that represent the strings and frets of the ukulele. This has the advantage of showing the player exactly where to place the fingers without prior knowledge of musical notation. Standard notation, however, is common to all musical instruments and, once learned, conveys more performance information than tablature alone. This will help you to experiment and choose alternative fingerings that may be more suitable for you individually than those shown in tablature.

• Organization by keys

This will help you to develop a sense of key families and relationships. Gradually you will learn to hear and play the patterns of harmony that bind the tunes together.

• Musical arrangements

41 pieces representative of many genres, classical, folk, pop, jazz and some new music specially composed for this book.

• Technical challenges

96 short studies to introduce new skills and ideas which are developed in the pieces.

• I Love Music

17 ways to sing and play my refreshed version of an old favorite, and providing at the same time a recurring motif (or binding thread) throughout the book.

• The anatomy of the ukulele

An illustrated chapter demonstrating the chord shapes and scales that can move all over the fingerboard and showing how the arrangements can be constructed by knowing where the notes are! Also discover some of the more outlandish secret moves held within the instrument's capabilities.

• Exercise framework

Just like going to the gym! Develop finger fitness with these 21 studies and at the same time gain confidence in making position changes on the fretboard.

• Recordings

All of the pieces, arrangements and studies in *Discovering Fingerstyle Ukulele* are available as Audio Downloads (labelled ▶ TRACK in the text).

• Technical terms

Some of the technical and/or musical terms used in *Discovering Fingerstyle Ukulele* which may be unfamiliar to the beginner are marked in **bold type** on their first appearance in the book and are listed and defined in the Glossary, Appendix 1.

Which ukulele is best for you?

The ukulele comes in four main sizes, three having the same tuning:
Soprano – the most common size and best for young children starting fingerstyle.

Concert – this is more suitable for older beginners with its slightly larger fingerboard on which to place larger fingers! However, some older players may still prefer to use the Soprano instrument to begin with. Same tuning as the Soprano and Tenor ukulele.

Tenor – larger still and perhaps better suited to playing solo melodic lines. The arrangements in *Discovering Fingerstyle Ukulele* use chord shapes to provide the harmony in which some fingers are kept static whilst others play the melody notes. This often involves stretching to reach the higher frets and may be more difficult on an instrument with a longer neck. The use of a low G can give the Tenor, as a melodic instrument, a wider compass. Same tuning as the Soprano and Concert ukulele.

Baritone – tuned like a guitar's top 4 strings and approaching a three-quarter size guitar. This is ideal for a guitarist wanting to join a ukulele group without having to learn new chord names. The difficulty of stretching with the left hand to find the notes is, however, increased to a greater degree than on the Tenor ukulele.

The ukulele's popularity stems partly from the notion that it is the easiest of instruments to play. In this book you will discover some of its often hidden delights, but these come only with the same degree of application that all music demands. I am sure, however, that you will find both the challenge and the results immensely rewarding, as I have done. So tune up and play on!

Colin Tribe

Chapter 1
Starting out

Holding the instrument

I prefer to use a strap to help hold the ukulele whether sitting or standing. I find the extra support given is essential to allow freedom of movement for both hands and arms.

Fig. 1

Fig. 2

Some players sit and rest the instrument on the left thigh, a position used by classical guitarists; I have also seen players use a thigh support to lift the instrument to a more comfortable position.

To simplify reading and to show fretting I have included Tablature staves TAB, a standard practice nowadays.

The ukulele has 4 strings which, when played open, sound the notes
G-C-E-A.

Fig. 3

G   C   E   A

This is not in the order you would expect if you have played guitar, mandolin or violin where the pitch rises from bottom to top string. Traditionally the G string on the ukulele is tuned an octave higher than you might expect. This is called a "re-entrant tuning" and is used throughout the book.

This tutor concentrates on fingerstyle playing which means making full use of the fingers of the right hand. If you are used to strumming chords with the thumb, first finger or plectrum this will slow you down at first, but persevere and the techniques will, through repetition, begin to feel natural.

Fig. 4

Play the strings with the right hand like this (and see Fig. 4):

G – 4th string with the thumb (***p***)
C – 3th string with the index finger (***i***)
E – 2nd string with the middle finger (***m***)
A – 1st string with the ring finger (***a***)

The letters are abbreviations of the Spanish names for the respective fingers and are universally used in guitar notation:

p = Pulgar = thumb
i = Indice = index finger
m = Medio = middle finger
a = Annular = ring finger

*You can download all audio tracks at: en.schott-music.com/fingerstyle-ukulele

The fingers should learn to feel for their own string and rest on it. When it is that string's turn to be played, gently pluck and come to a stop in mid-air, not coming to rest on the string above it. This is called a free stroke. The hand should stay relatively still – only the fingers and thumb move.

Left-hand fingers are shown as numbers 1 2 3 4.

At the end of this chapter is a full notation and tablature chart to help you locate notes on the ukulele fretboard and to help you find alternative fingerings if some are uncomfortable for you.

For the first studies you will need to learn the following note values; listen to the recording downloads to help you hear what you see and it will gradually become easier.

♩ = 1 beat; a quarter note (crotchet)
♪ = a half beat; an eighth note (quaver)
𝅗𝅥 = 2 beats; a half note (minim)

The 4/4 time signature indicates that each measure (bar) will contain the equivalent of 4 quarter notes; I have included a counting line to help you.

Study 1

Support the neck of the ukulele with your left hand; place the thumb behind the neck under the 2nd fret with the fingers loosely curled above – but not touching – any of the strings.

Colin Tribe

Study 2

This study introduces the note F: 1st finger on the 1st fret of the 2nd string. Make sure the 1st finger forms an arch so that it does not touch the A or C strings. Keep the left hand thumb in its most normal place; resting on the neck behind the 2nd fret. For this, use the right-hand fingers *i m* in a walking pattern as shown. I have started with *m*, as this is the usual finger that plays play the E string but starting with *i* is perfectly acceptable.

▶ TRACK 3

CT

The Westminster Chimes

This is perhaps the most well-known 4-note piece of music in the world; in my arrangement each note is played on a different string.

It may be because it was constructed by a clock maker rather than a musician that it has an unusual timing of 5 beats in each measure – until the chimes at the end for which there are 3 beats as each hour is chimed.

I have chosen to set the piece at 8 o'clock, but you could choose any hour you like by varying the number of chimes at the end.

To sound the chimes, the right hand plucks all 4 strings at the same time. I call this a *pinch*: the thumb moves downwards whilst the other fingers move up. A new note length is used for the chime: the dotted half note (minim) ♩. worth 3 beats.

The Westminster Chimes

► TRACK 4

CT

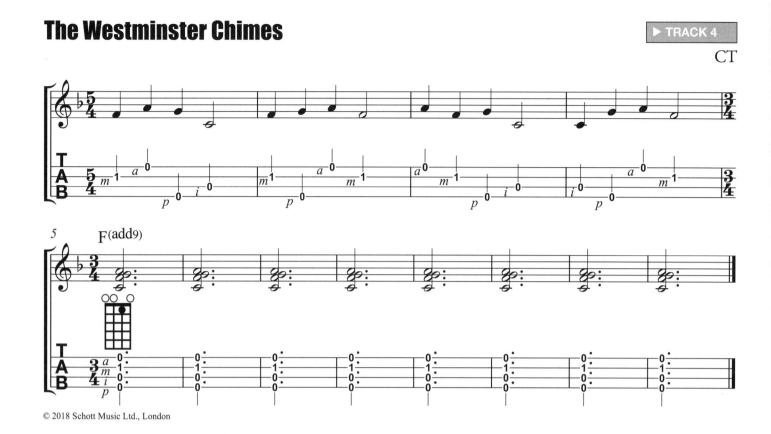

F(add9)

The chord for the chimes is quite unusual and may not be one you will have come across when accompanying songs. It is called an "Fadd9". The F gives you the normal 3-note chord (or **Triad**) of F major which is: F – A – C (the 1st, 3rd and 5th notes of the F scale), whilst the G is the 9th note of the F scale – the "added 9th".

Some clock makers miss out the G but I love the musical clash it produces!

Notice in the photograph (Fig. 5) that the arched finger and the fingertip are just touching the string, emphasizing the need for short nails on your left hand, although for the right hand I like to have a nail length that gives a bit of a bite to the string being plucked!

Fig. 5

Here is a full notation and tablature chart to help you locate notes on the ukulele fretboard and to help you find alternative fingerings if mine are too uncomfortable for you:

Fig. 6

Chapter 2
Tunes using the short scale of C

On many instruments you will start by learning tunes in the key of C major, which are the eight white notes on the piano between two C's at any octave. As the lowest note of the ukulele is C – the same as middle C on the piano – I think it is good place to begin.

Study 1

This study introduces the five notes of the short scale of C.
Note the **repeat sign,** a double bar with double dots

$\|$: and :$\|$

▶ TRACK 5

CT

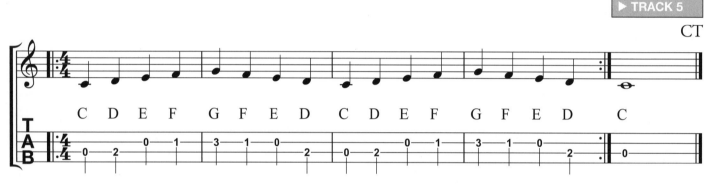

Right hand: use the finger-walking pattern with *i m* shown in Chapter 1, Study 2.
Left hand: use finger 1 at fret 1, finger 2 at fret 2, and finger 3 at fret 3.

Study 2

This study uses the notes of the short C scale together with some of the rhythms you have learned so far.

▶ TRACK 6

CT

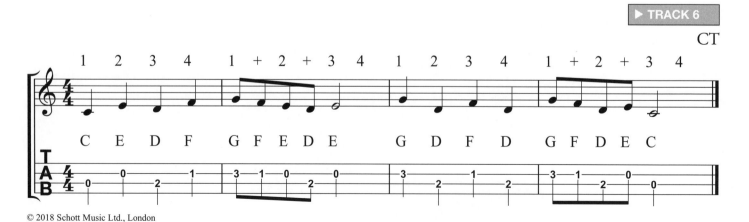

When The Saints Go Marching In

This famous tune uses the five notes of the short C major scale. Listen to yourself play and make sure you are getting a good sound from each note. I have included a counting line; the time signature is **cut time** (music symbol ₵) which has a count and feel of two half note beats in each measure.

The quarter rest sign 𝄽 therefore indicates a silence for half a beat.

When The Saints Go Marching In

▶ TRACK 7

American Traditional
Arr. Colin Tribe

Study 3

In this study add a **drone** on the open G 4th string played with the thumb; use the other fingers as indicated.

Use a *pima* pinch to play a C chord at the end as in *The Westminster Chimes*.

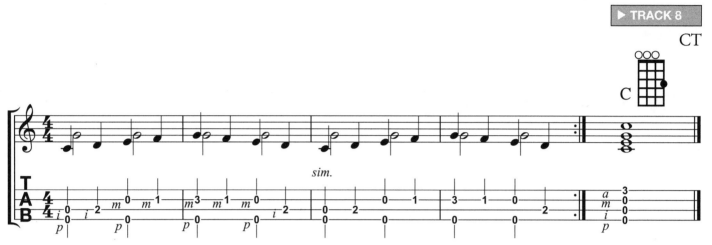

© 2018 Schott Music Ltd., London

Renaissance Dance

Use finger 1 at fret 1, finger 2 at fret 2, and finger 3 at fret 3. For the note D in measures 10, 11, 14, and 15 use the 3rd finger tucked under the 2nd which will sound A on the G string at fret 2.

The right-hand thumb plays the open G string; use the walking pattern *i m* on other notes. The repeat is managed with a 1st and 2nd time bar. Listen to the Audio Download to understand what is happening.

Renaissance Dance

▶ TRACK 9

Tylman Susato (c. 1510–c. 1570)
Arr. Colin Tribe

Chapter 3
Tunes in C minor

Study 1

This study includes some new notes with the **flat** sign ♭; the sign is placed to the left of a note and indicates that the note is to be lowered in pitch by one half step (semitone). You will also learn to use the 4th finger at fret 4. Fingerstyle ukulele playing uses the little finger a lot, so begin to make it strong!

▶ TRACK 10

Study 2

This study introduces a new rhythm: a dotted eighth note ♪. followed by a sixteenth ♪; this is an important feature of the melody *Play Around* and gives a skipping effect. Here you can learn to distinguish it from a pair of eighth notes.

▶ TRACK 11

The diagram below shows the notes and their names on the first five frets of the ukulele. The lowest note playable is middle C. To help orientation, you could write the note names in the piano keyboard diagram shown at the bottom. The piano layout offers the simplest way of understanding musical notes.

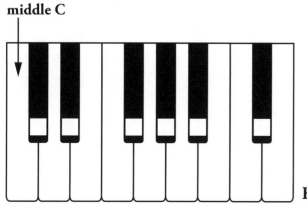

Fig. 7

Another note locator

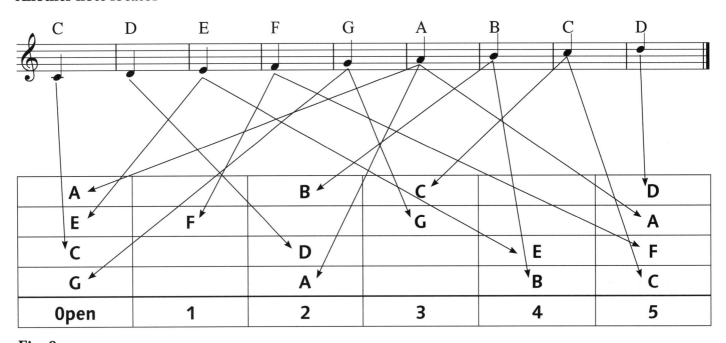

Fig. 8

The next piece, *Play Around,* is a march with two beats per measure with a **time signature** of 2/4, each beat representing a marching leg! It is in C minor, a key with three flats; the **key signature** shows the notes affected are B♭, E♭ and A♭.

You might recognize the tune as a slower, sadder version of *Frères Jacques* which Mahler borrowed and changed for this funeral setting in his First Symphony. It works very well as a **round** with each player (or singer) beginning at 4-measure intervals as indicated, so when the first player gets to measure 5 the next player starts at measure 1. Note the drone effect on the G string as in *Renaissance Dance*.

Play Around

▶ TRACK 12

(Theme from Symphony No. 1)

Gustav Mahler (1860–1911)
Arr. Colin Tribe

Much of the music in this book is grouped according to the key of the pieces. This is to systematically introduce you to the musical families. The left hand will play chord shapes and scale passages associated with the keys and these will be learned through repetition. I will include scales and the new chord shapes needed to play the pieces and studies for you to practice.

Study 3

This is the C harmonic minor scale. Use the same finger as the respective fret. It will help strengthen the 4th (little) finger.

▶ TRACK 13

CT

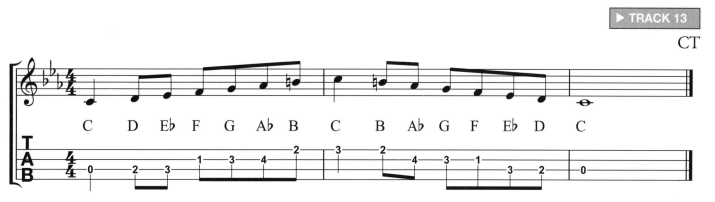

Study 4

Here is the C harmonic minor scale with an added drone G played with the thumb. G is the 5th note of the scale of C and is called the **dominant**.

▶ TRACK 14

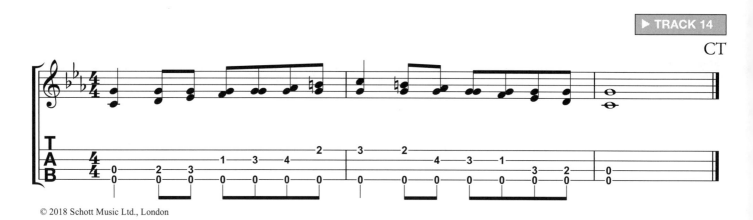

"The Blues" is a well-known musical form and the term is used in music to encompass many aspects both social and musical. I am using it here:

• to indicate the chord sequence which accompanies the tune - known as the **12-bar blues**.

• to show the use of the flattened 3rd and 7th from the scale of C: the notes **E♭** and **B♭**.

• to demonstrate the typical blues rhythmic feel called **"Swing"**; this means that pairs of eighth notes are not equal, the first being longer than the second. It is similar to the dotted rhythm in *Play Around* but split two-thirds to one-third rather than three-quarters to one-quarter.

Blues in C

▶ TRACK 15

Colin Tribe

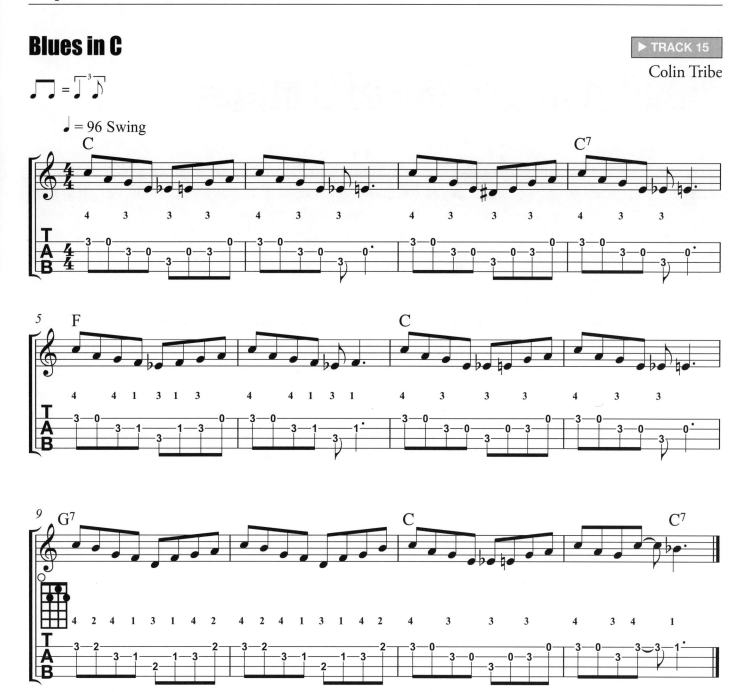

© 2018 Schott Music Ltd., London

Use an alternating right-hand *i m* pattern for this melody. Follow the left-hand fingerings as indicated. In measures 9 and 10, hold a G7 chord shape as shown in the diagram and just add the little finger where indicated – it makes a lovely pattern as it moves across the strings.

We will revisit this *Blues in C* in the next chapter when you will learn to add an accompaniment to it.

Chapter 4
Playing in the key of C major

In this chapter you will start using chords to accompany the melody being played. Many of the chords will be just as you would use them in Sing and Strum Sessions, but often only part of the chord will be used to make way for the melody.

Study 1
The scale of C major

This is the most ukulele friendly scale, so prepare to have it at your fingertips!
Learn the note names as you practice it.

▶ TRACK 16

CT

Study 2

This study is a short two-chord tune of mine *La la la la la* which uses parts of the C and G7 chords to accompany the melody. Repeat it many times!

I originally wrote it as a song to amuse my grandson Edward and it had these words:

Mummy sings a song it goes La la la la la,
Edward sings a song it goes La la la la la
Nan T sings a song it goes La la la la la,
Dziadzia sings a song it goes La la la la la

The first three are beautifully done but the one by *Dziadzia*[*] is loud, out of tune and horrible!

---
[*] *Dziadzia* is the Polish for Grandfather

► TRACK 17

Colin Tribe

Casey Jones

A short chromatic run on the A string starts the piece rolling; note the "Swing" feel indicated for this American folk tune about an early super-hero!

The G at the end of measure 14 is a new chord shape **0 2 3 5**; an alternative **4 2 3 5** could be tried to give a fuller sound if you can manage it.

The G sharp on fret 4 in measure 6 might be a bit of a stretch; you can substitute G on the 3rd fret if you need to but, whichever you choose, play the note with the 4th finger.

Casey Jones

▶ TRACK 18

American Traditional
Arr. Colin Tribe

Study 3

For the next piece you will need to play harmonized notes. The intervals in this study are called "thirds".

Left-hand fingerings are shown and notice the two different ways of playing the E–G interval.

Right hand: use *i m* together.

▶ TRACK 19

CT

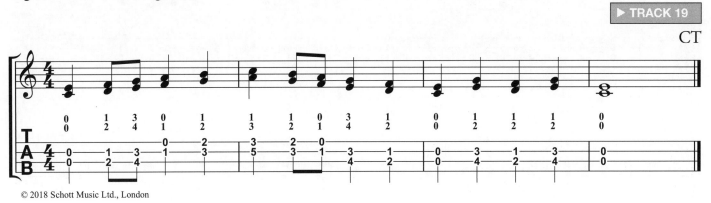

Study 4

An essential skill is to play with *p* and *i* alternating on the G and C strings. Practice this study in preparation for the next piece.

▶ TRACK 20

CT

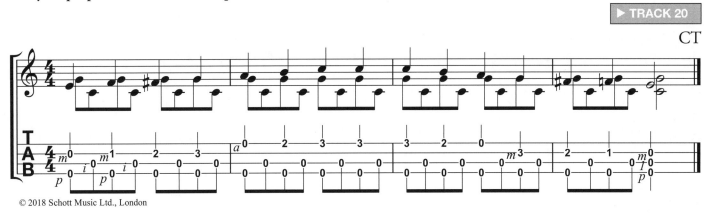

Pay Me My Money Down

Although it only has two chords, C and G7, there are some tricky rhythms in this piece typical of Caribbean Islands' music. I have put in a counting line to help with some of the syncopations.

Listening to the Audio Track will make the rhythms clear.

I have put in two alternative fingerings for the left hand:

• below the notes – same finger as the fret; this is an excellent workout for the 3rd and 4th fingers but might take some doing at first!

• above the notes – sliding between 1st position and 3rd position; use fingers 1 and 2 for the first notes of the piece.

D.C.al fine (Italian: *Da capo al fine*) means go back to the beginning and end at **Fine.**

Pay Me My Money Down

▶ TRACK 21

Caribbean Traditional
Arr. Colin Tribe

Fine

D.C. al Fine

Brahms's Lullaby

This piece has more of the alternate strokes with *p* and *i* that you used in the last tune and practiced in Study 3. The line joining the notes in measure 15 indicates that you slide from one fret to the next, and in this case you are holding two notes at once as played in Study 2. Note the little finger is suggested for fingering the F chord in measures 10 and 14. Using 3 is possible but the hand shape is more flexible with 4.

I have also used a **hammer-on** in measure13 and **pull-offs** in 16. These are not essential but do give a subtle musical effect called **legato**. Use them when you feel confident after working on Study 4 which is based on the pentatonic (5-note) scale of C.

The technique is to play with the right hand only the first of each pair of notes. In a "hammer-on" you then bring down the fretting finger with enough force to make the new note sound. In the more difficult "pull-off" you release the fretting finger, but in doing so, give the string a slight snap with that finger so as to play the next note.

Study 5

▶ TRACK 22

CT

Lullaby

► TRACK 23

Johannes Brahms (1833–1897)
Arr. Colin Tribe

Slow and gentle (♩ = 72)

Study 6

The right-hand pattern in this study demonstrates a very important technique, so be prepared to practice this study several times to get used to the feel of the finger movements.

The final C chord can be played in several ways; try these suggestions as you repeat the piece:

- play all four strings simultaneously in a *pima pluck* - a pinching movement.

- play a very fast arpeggio, starting with *p* on the G string; I call this a *pima roll*.

- play a slower arpeggio where you can hear the individual notes: a *slow pima roll*.

- play a fast sweep across the strings with the back of the nails.

  I use index, middle, ring and little finger in that order: *i m a l*

  16 notes are sounded as each nail brushes across each string.

  Experiment with this, it takes a while for it to sound effective; I call it a *nail brush.*

▶ TRACK 24

CT

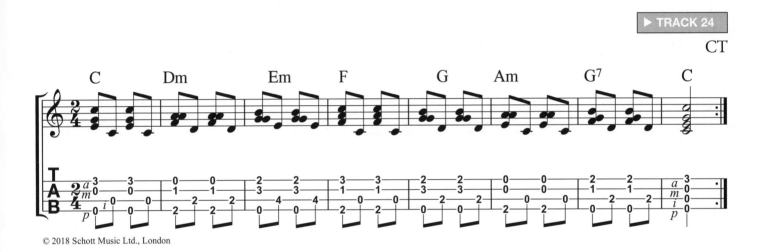

Dziadzia's Tune

This piece includes all three of the minor chords that can be formed from the notes of the C major scale: A minor, D minor and E minor.

Dziadzia's Tune

(Grandfather's Tune)   Colin Tribe

Now let's return to *Blues in C*, a tune learned in chapter 3. This time we add a chord accompaniment on the first beat of each measure except at the end which is syncopated. Note the repeats with 1st and 2nd time measures. Try to use a ***pima*** pluck or roll on the chords and try to make them sound for the whole measure.

Blues in C

(with chords)

▶ TRACK 26

Colin Tribe

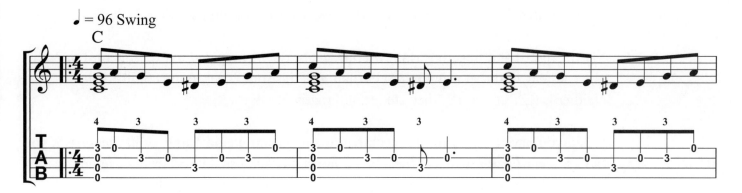

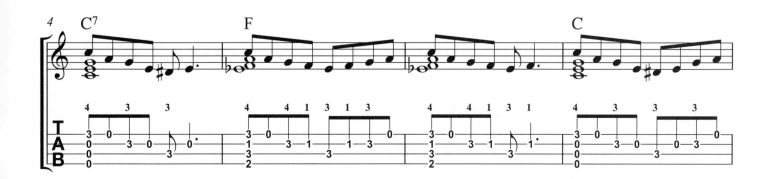

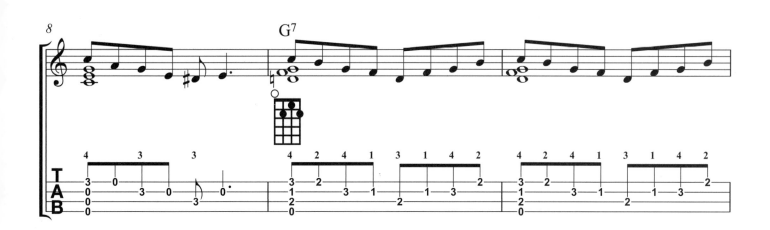

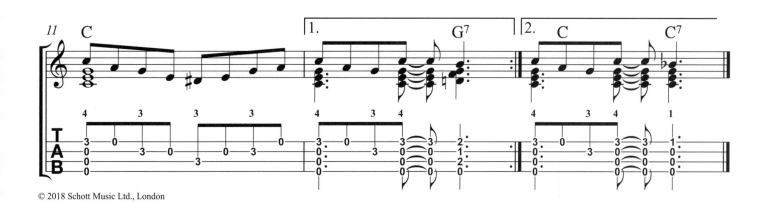

Wooden Heart

The next piece, *Wooden Heart*, is adapted from a German traditional tune "Muss i' den" ("Must I then"), famously sung by Elvis Presley in the hit film *G.I.Blues* (1960).

Try the right-hand fingering as shown but, as always, be prepared to experiment. For example, you may find that using *m* rather than *a* in measure 2 feels more comfortable. Neither is right or wrong, they are just alternatives.

When you have a chord in the accompaniment but no melody note, as in measure 5, you can use a *nail brush* stroke rather than a *pima* pluck. I use the nail of my *i* finger mainly, but experiment with others. Try to keep it soft so that the melody will ring out. I have shown the stroke with a vertical wavy line .

Experiment with left-hand fingering in measures 21–22; hold the G on the 2nd string as you change the notes on the 3rd and 4th strings.

The ending has a strum that I regularly use as standard when playing chords.

In measure 31 I *pima* pluck the first beat then use *nail brush* strokes with individual fingers. The index fingernail strums physically down from the G towards the A and the thumbnail strums physically up from the A to the G. It may be confusing at first to use the terms "up" and "down", as the direction of the arrowhead is opposite to what you might expect – but the terms are musically correct as the top string is at the bottom of the instrument!

Wooden Heart

("Muss i' denn")

▶ TRACK 27

German Traditional
Arr. Colin Tribe

Chapter 5
Playing in the key of F major

Now it's time to work on a tune that everyone should learn to play for themselves on at least one special day of the year: *Happy Birthday to You*!

Study 1

Practice moving to the chord of B flat, a tricky position found in measure 15.

G = 3rd, C = 2nd, E = 1st, A = 1st

Fig. 9

This hand position defeats many players for a while, with its double stop on strings 1 and 2, both played with the 1st finger.

This study also works on the technique of tucking in the 3rd finger on the C string under the 2nd finger on the G string as, for example, in measure 10 of *Happy Birthday to You*.

Use this study to experiment further with different ways of playing the *pima* stroke.

▶ TRACK 28

CT

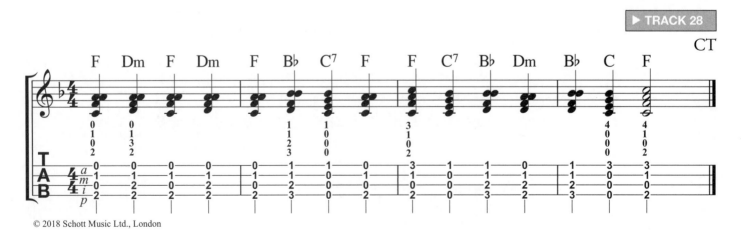

Study 2

This study will further help you play tucking the 3rd finger under the 2nd.

The second measure of the study will help you practice the important fingering used in measure 12 of *Happy Birthday*, where the 3rd and 4th fingers need to be at the same fret but a string apart. Make sure you can hear the open C sounding.

I have used three strings (until the final measure), use *p i m* for the first three measures and *p i m a* for the final one.

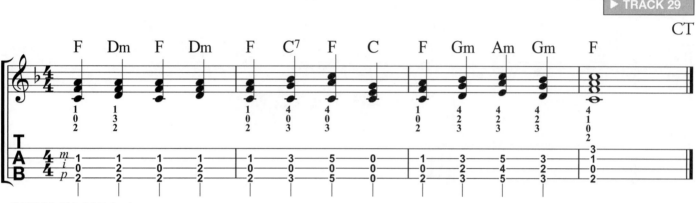

© 2018 Schott Music Ltd., London

Happy Birthday to You

I have arranged this so that the first time through you just play the melody; add in the chord harmonies when it is repeated.

Measure 14 has two important features:

• the sound of the first chord in the measure has E and B flat sounding together giving the interval of a flattened 5th which has a lovely tension; this is resolved when the E melody note falls to a D.

• the B flat chord on the final beat fingered 3 2 1 1 which is a short way to indicate strings and frets:

G = 3rd C = 2nd E = 1st A = 1st

Happy Birthday to You

▶ TRACK 30

American Traditional
Arr. Colin Tribe

Study 3

An important technique is introduced in this study. In measure 1 the little finger needs to play the D on the 5th fret of the A string whilst you hold the basic F shape 2 0 1 on the G-C-E strings.

From the start of this tutor I have emphasized the need for a flexible left-hand little finger: this will test it out!

Notice that in measure 2 I use the 4th finger on the 3rd fret A string straight after the 3rd finger plays the 3rd fret on the E string. It will sound good if you continue to hold the 3rd finger in place whilst playing with the 4th.

Generally my arrangements encourage you to hold notes for as long as possible; use your ears to listen to the effect and then your musicality to decide if you want that effect.

▶ TRACK 31

CT

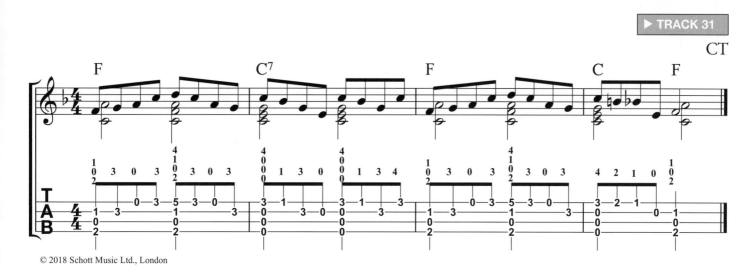

O Tannenbaum

A two-chord song this time using the **tonic** F and its **dominant** partner C7.

Music can often be seen as a journey from the chord based on the key note or tonic (in this case the keynote is F and its chord has the notes F-A-C) and the chord based on the fifth note of the scale, called the dominant 7th (in this case it is C7 which has the notes C-E-G-B♭).

Note the use of dotted eighths/sixteenths and equal eighth note pairs, just like in *Play Around* in Chapter 2.

Be flexible about using fingers 3 and 4 and aim to keep your hand comfortable; if you are practicing a lot, you do not want to cause too much strain.

For the melody, try a walking alternating *i m* pattern.

O Tannenbaum

(O Christmas Tree)

▶ TRACK 32

German Traditional
Arr. Colin Tribe

Mango Walk

This piece uses the same chords – F and C7 – as *O Tannenbaum*.

Notice the syncopated melody rhythm in measures 2–4 and later; the accompaniment, however, stays firmly on the beat.

I play the first chord F with fingers 2, 1 and 4. In the second measure move the 1st finger to fret 3 which will help you to reach fret 5 with the 3rd finger; then move the 1st finger back to play the B flat.

I use finger 4 on the C in measures 4 and 8. I choose this option as it makes the hand shape more compact. But it is always important to experiment to ensure that it is comfortable for you as a player.

Mango Walk

▶ TRACK 33

Caribbean Traditional
Arr. Colin Tribe

Study 4

Here is another version of the B♭ chord that is a stretch, needing careful hand and wrist positioning to enable 4th finger to reach the D on the A string at the 5th fret.

To play the F chord in measure 7 I have introduced a barre at the 5th fret. This needs some care to play and alert listening to make sure that you are making good contact with the 1st finger to sound each note. In this regard fingerstyle playing is more exacting than strumming since you cannot hide dull notes with good ones played at the same time; each note has its own space and needs to ring true.

▶ TRACK 34

CT

Deck the Halls

Note the natural sign ♮ in measure 11 which counteracts the flat ♭ in the key signature.

The strummed ending is similar to that in *Wooden Heart* from Chapter 4, but change from strum to **p i m** for the last two chords.

Deck the Halls

► TRACK 35

Traditional English Christmas Song
Arr. Colin Tribe

I Love Music 1

Now I want to introduce a piece that will reappear in different versions throughout this book.

It shows how the same piece can be rearranged to give it a new sound; hopefully this will encourage you to experiment with some of the ideas used in other pieces as you learn to play.

The best way to get to the heart of a piece of music is to sing it … so listen to my daughter Tania sing on Audio Track 36 and join in!

1. Sing the melody

This uses new words to the tune *Frère Jacques* or *I Hear Thunder*.

If you are working with a teacher or friends, then sing it as a round, entry points are shown here with boxed numbers. Chords are shown in capital letters, but it is better to sing and not play at first.

I Love Music 1

▶ TRACK 36

French Traditional
Arr. Colin Tribe

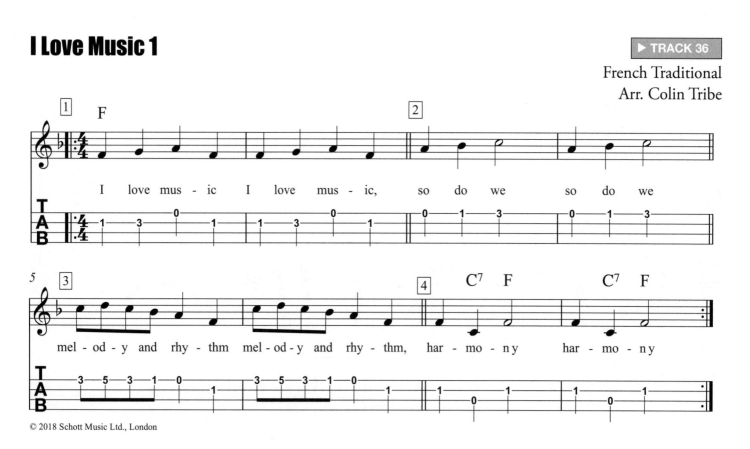

I Love Music 2

2. Play the melody

Experiment with your right-hand fingerings; alternating index *i* and middle *m* fingers as indicated is a good starting point, but you can play *i* on 1st string and then on 2nd string when it follows straight after and then go on to *m*.

You should also explore the difference between free strokes (ending in the air) and rest strokes (ending on the next string).

I have put in note names to help you to know where things are. For the note B flat (♭) sing or say B flat. See "Fat Fish note names" in Appendix 2 for the complete set.

I Love Music 2

▶ TRACK 37

Arr. CT

I Love Music 3

3. Play the melody with harmony

A chord is played on the first beat of each measure or at harmony change.

The chord should remain in position throughout the measure to provide the continuing harmony, often using fingers in unusual ways that will take some getting used to:

• two fingers on the same string

• double stopping – one finger on two strings

• difficult stretches.

The arrows ↓ point to those features; they also show where I use just part of chord in the two closing measures.

I Love Music 3

▶ TRACK 38

Arr. CT

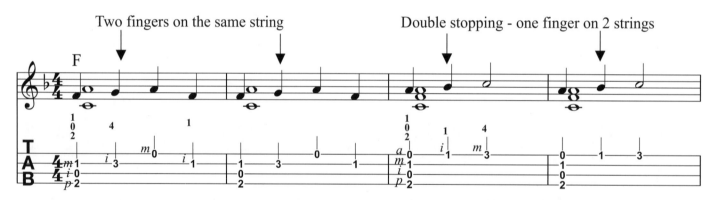

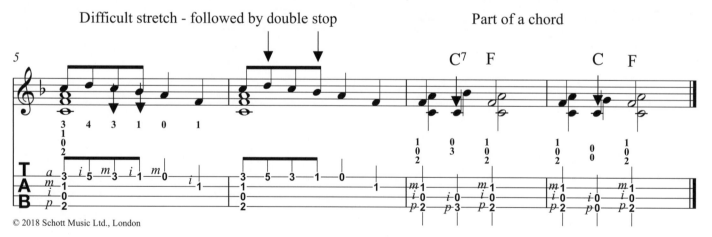

Chapter 6
Playing in the key of G major

Study 1

Here is a variation of the G major scale, starting on the 5th note of the scale (the dominant, 'D') instead of the 1st (the tonic, 'G').

It does not use open strings, and because the 1st finger is at fret 2 throughout it is marked as being in II position. The final G chord will take getting used to; it uses all four fingers and produces a very full sound, as each note is different.

▶ TRACK 39

CT

II position

Study 2

To prepare for the next tune *First Love*, here is a study showing different fingerings that enable the 4th finger to reach fret 5 whilst still holding the chords of G, D or D7.

Measure 1: this starts with the standard G chord fingering and then adding 4th finger at fret 3 to play a C and then twisting the hand to enable that finger to play fret 4 C♯.

Measure 2: the G is played substituting the 2nd for 3rd finger on the E string 3rd fret and barring with the 1st finger across the C-E-A strings so it is ready to play the final B. I can play the C on fret 3 as a double stop with my 2nd finger (which has become very flexible over the years), but if yours doesn't bend backwards yet, you can just move the 2nd finger from 2nd string to 1st!

Measure 3: there are many choices of fingering when playing D [2 2 2 0]. By using various combinations of fingers and thumb I found 32 ways of doing it, but only about 6 are really useful!

The version shown here uses a double stop with 1st finger; a common way for classical guitarists.

Measure 2: to follow the fingering shown, use a double stop with finger 2 on the C – if that is too difficult, swap to finger 3 for that note and slide it down from fret 4 to the C♯.

Measure 4: lift the 1st finger so that it allows the C string to sound open and you should be able to reach the 5th fret D with the 4th finger.

Measure 5: as an ending chord I have used G at VII position – a barre chord as in the Coda of *First Love*. Try shifting the 1st finger around to find the best contact on the 7th fret.

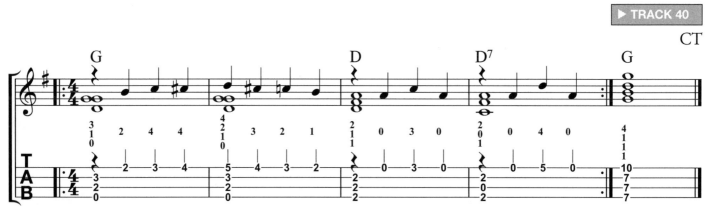

First Love

▶ TRACK 41

Colin Tribe

To Coda

Coda

D.C. al Coda

Study 3

Introducing new chord shapes and fingerings for *Swing Low, Sweet Chariot.*

▶ TRACK 42

CT

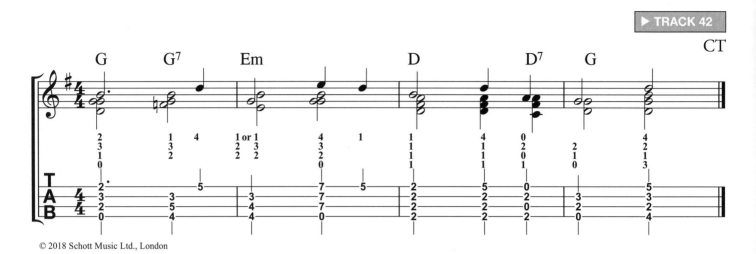

Swing Low, Sweet Chariot

▶ TRACK 43

American Traditional
Arr. Colin Tribe

D.S. al Coda

In *Careless Love* try out the brush stroke to play chords when no melody notes are being played; this will be quite a lot of the time as the melody is slow moving!

Careless Love

▶ TRACK 44

Colin Tribe

Sloop John B begins with a 4-measure claves rhythm melodic riff. The accompanying chords are on the beat with the melody syncopating around it; be careful, though, as the melody does not just repeat itself. I have put in a time line to help.

Notice the D chord fingering in measure 11. This is how Buddy Holly played the shape on guitar for *Peggy Sue* and I have always liked its flexibility; but it might feel a bit of a squash at first.

Raise the wrist so the fingers are arched over with just fingertips touching the strings.

Sloop John B

▶ TRACK 45

Bahamas Traditional
Arr. Colin Tribe

Study 4

Suo-Gân (Lullaby) is a traditional Welsh tune used in the film *Empire of the Sun*. It has some lovely rich harmonies and introduces new versions of E minor as well as new two chords, B minor and Dsus4. Here is a study putting them in the context of the scale notes and chords of G major.

B minor is a tricky shape with the need for a barre at the 2nd fret with the 2nd or 3rd finger on the G string 4th fret. You can leave out the note on the G string if it stops you playing the tune. I have included an **ossia** or alternative measure in the study to show how that would work.

▶ TRACK 46

CT

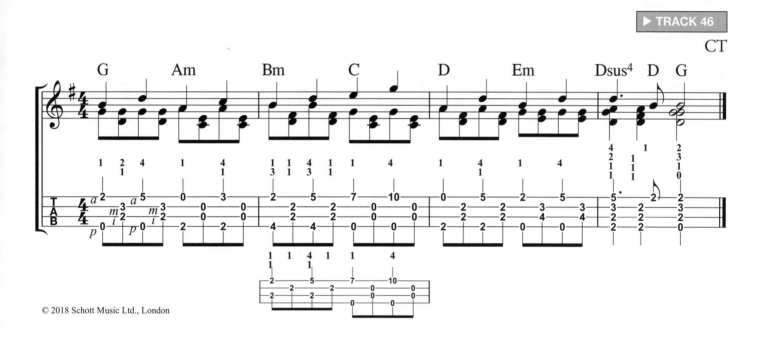

As *Suo-Gân* is often played on a Welsh harp, this piece could employ **arpeggios** (which means sounding as a harp) using a *pima* roll.

To play these, the fingers pluck one after the other rather than simultaneously. Ideally the fingers should be positioned on their own designated string and be ready to play as soon as the previous string has been plucked. It is a difficult technique at first but is one that the right hand can practice with any chord or open strings when your left hand is feeling too tired for other things!

On the Audio Track I repeat the piece three times and add the arpeggios in the first and last playing. Listen to the difference between the versions and then judge for yourself the speed and frequency of using them or not.

Suo-Gân

(Lullaby)

♩ = 72

Welsh Traditional
Arr. Colin Tribe

▶ TRACK 47

I Love Music 4

Playing the melody in Campanella style

Here the tune is arranged so that successive notes are played on different strings. This allows the notes to carry on ringing for as long as possible and merging into each other as in bell ringing, hence the name *Campanella*.

I have put in a slide in measures 7 and 8. After playing the 5th fret note, slide the 2nd finger down the string till you reach the 2nd fret, then lift it off with a slight pluck with that finger as it leaves the string. Alternatively, let the finger leave the string after it passes the nut.

I Love Music 4

▶ TRACK 48

CT

I Love Music 5

Chord solo

In this style the harmony is played as a chord together with the melody note. By using a *pima* roll for this, beginning with the thumb on the G string and followed rapidly with as many fingers as you need out of *i m a.* The melody note, which is generally on the highest string, will be played slightly after the other notes and so will stand out.

I Love Music 5

▶ TRACK 49

CT

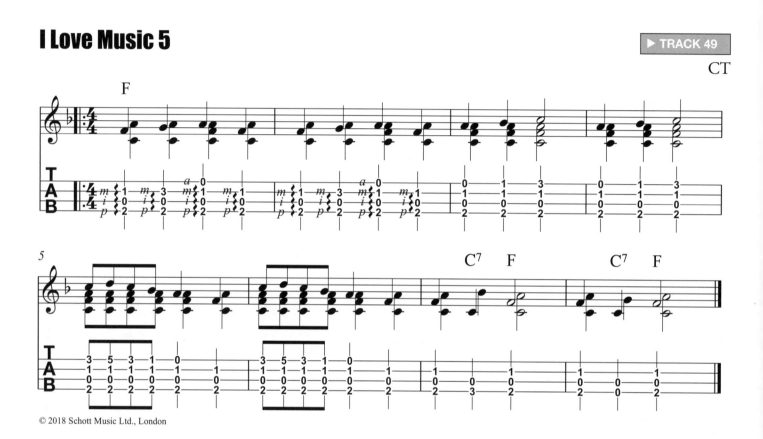

Chapter 7
Playing in the key of A minor

Study 1

The key of A minor is the relative minor of C major and it shares the same key signature (no sharps, no flats). The harmonic minor version of the scale has the leading note sharpened, and so G♯ is written in the music as an accidental.

This study shows three ways of playing the one octave scale of A harmonic minor, the octave of the first note 'A' being found on the 12th fret.

• measures 1–4: all on the A string; note the hand position changes just once.

• measures 5–8: in Campanella style like *I Love Music 4* in chapter 6; a strange hand feeling to this at first, but try my fingering before maybe developing your own. Try to allow sounds to continue and so blend together.

• measures 9–13: this is the standard pattern for all the harmonic minor scales from C♯ minor to A minor. Note that the 1st finger is used at two different frets.

This study ends with a tricky A minor chord **9 9 8 12.** I double stop the bottom two strings with 2nd finger, but using all four fingers is fine; just make sure of a high arched hand to make room for the fingers. The higher up the frets, the closer they are together as you will have noticed!

Here are pictures of the alternative ways of fingering **9 9 8 12**

Fig. 10   **Fig. 11**

▶ TRACK 50
CT

Study 2

This is a chord study to help familiarize yourself with the versions of the three main chords in the key of A minor: Am, Dm and E7 (chords made up entirely of notes from the A minor scale). Chords from the middle section in C major are also used in the piece, but they should be familiar to you by now.

▶ TRACK 51
CT

Study 3

At times it is very useful to play in octaves; this study uses them as in my arrangement of the
Song of the Volga Boatmen.

▶ TRACK 52

CT

© 2018 Schott Music Ltd., London

Song of the Volga Boatmen

▶ TRACK 53

Russian Traditional
Arr. Colin Tribe

Study 4

After an easy opening the next piece *The Eagle*, has a tough section starting with the Dm in measure 9; I have included a simpler ossia (alternative section) if you need to use it. Don't feel bad about doing that, everyone's skills develop at a different pace and the main written part might not feel comfortable for a while longer. Remember that all this is designed to be enjoyable so don't push yourself too hard!

Here is a study to help overcome two awkward manoeuvres. First, the 3-string barre in measures 1 and 2 and then the movement of the 4th finger while holding the C and then B♭ chord.

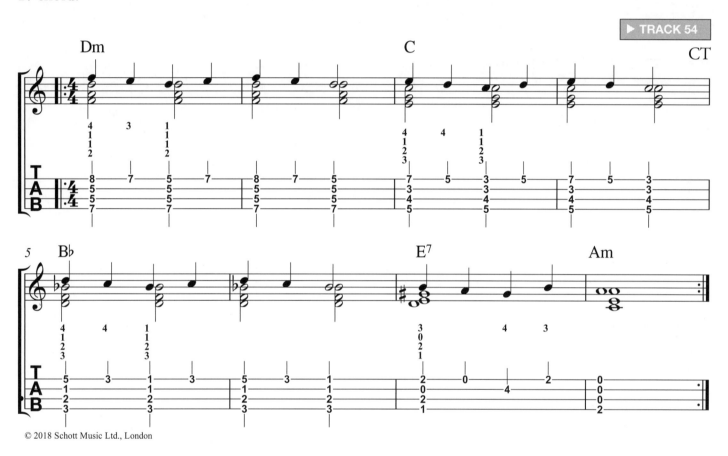

Study 5

I use a 3-string barre in measure 17, the first of the Coda measures. The difficulty here is to let the open A string ring true. In this study I also use the 1st finger to fret the A string to let you develop the flexibility of the 1st finger.

The Eagle

▶ TRACK 56

Colin Tribe

To Coda

Coda

D.S. al Coda

I Love Music 6

Melody with alternating strings accompaniment

In this style the accompanying harmony is played with *p i* patterns on the G and C strings.

I Love Music 6

▶ TRACK 57

I Love Music 7

Chords with embedded melody

The chords are played with a rhythmic strum. The melody notes are, of course, included, but are not given prominence. I often use this style in repeats since the melody will already have been established. Melody notes can also be repeated in the strums without spoiling the effect.

Either mute the unused strings with left-hand fingers or miss them out with accurate right-hand strumming.

My usual strum technique uses the back of the nails and follows the pattern: "Down with *i*, up with *p*".

I Love Music 7   ▶ TRACK 58

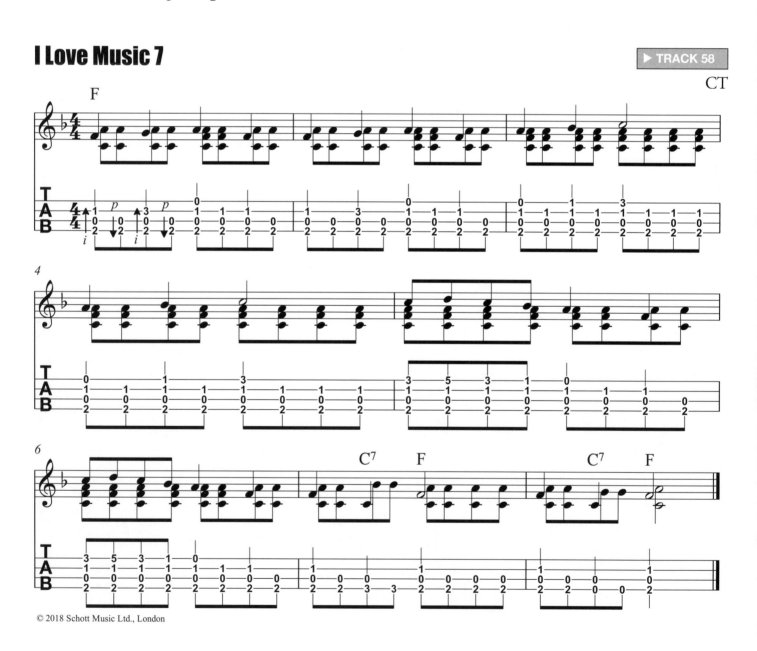

Chapter 8
Playing in the key of G minor

Malagueña is a well-known Spanish guitar piece that translates very well to the ukulele. I have included it in the G minor chapter but it is modal in character as is much folk music. It includes several different playing techniques; I have separated the music into six sections to learn before you put them together in the complete piece.

Study 1

The first four measures are played with the 1st finger moving from string to string and giving a staccato effect, effectively cutting each note in half. Each note is played with the thumb. This has been marked in the tab staff.

In measures 5–8 play with a barre and right-hand fingers as shown to give a **legato** effect, indicated by the slur line in the music staff. Let the notes last as long as possible; in bars 5 and 6 let them ring and blend to become part of the chord.

▶ TRACK 59

CT

Study 2

Begin with a 1st finger barre for two measures with the little finger anchored at the 5th fret throughout. Play the right hand as shown ***p a*** throughout, except ***p i m a*** for the final chord.

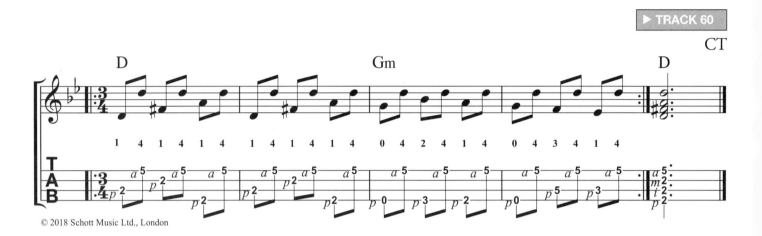

© 2018 Schott Music Ltd., London

Study 3

Use the right-hand fingering with rest strokes so that the plucking finger comes to rest on the next string. This can be a more forceful stroke than the regular free stroke and suits this single-note melody line.

In measure 4 use a **hammer-on** (h) and **pull-off** (p) to get a super legato effect; use a right-hand stroke for the first note of the measure.

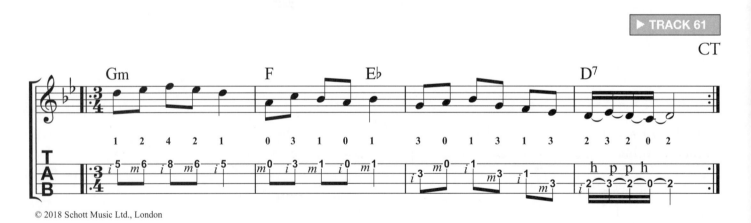

© 2018 Schott Music Ltd., London

Study 4

This is similar to Study 2 but with the addition of a right-hand **tremolo** figure. This should be practiced until it is as smooth and as fast as you can make it. The final chord is played with the nails brushing across the strings – *l* indicates little finger – each one hitting all four strings in rapid succession.

▶ TRACK 62

CT

Study 5

This section was one I "composed", but it is based on a well-used chord sequence found in numerous other traditional sources. Use the open G string to enrich the harmonies.

If you only have 12 frets then a slight bend will get the B♭ in measure 1. Try to sustain the chord on the first beat of each measure whilst the melody is played.

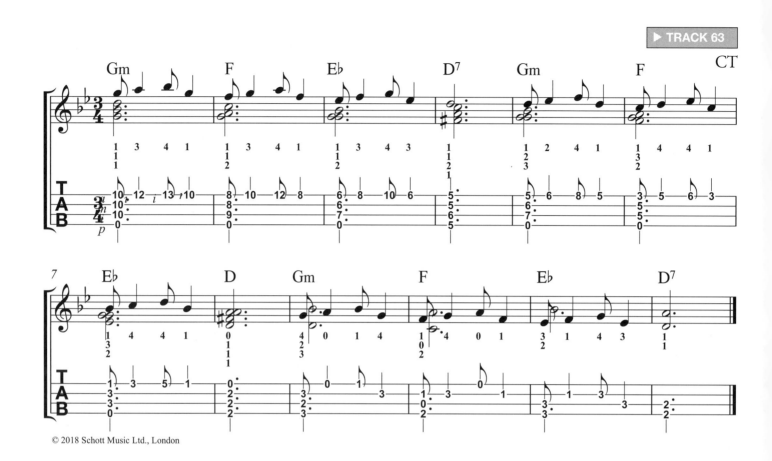

Study 6

Begin this closing chordal section softly with the fleshy part of the thumb playing down strokes, moving to nail strokes when *i* comes in with alternate up and down strokes. End with the Nail Brush as in Study 4. As indicated, it gets louder and faster till the climactic G minor. You could repeat measures 5-8 four times to make the **crescendo** and **accelerando** even more gradual and dramatic.

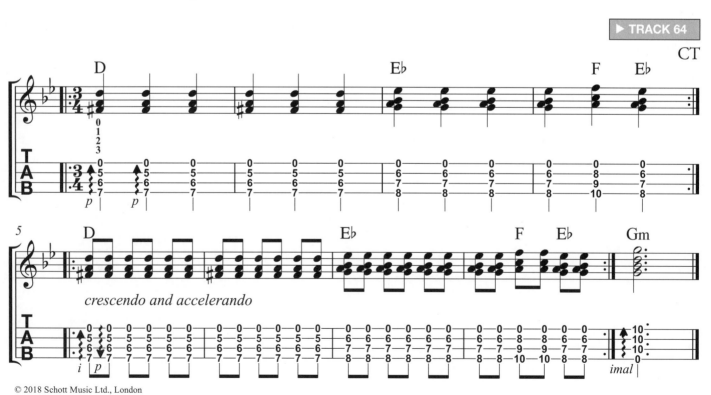

Malagueña

▶ TRACK 65

Spanish Traditional
Arr. Colin Tribe

Coventry Carol

The *Coventry Carol* dates from the 16th century and was traditionally performed in Coventry*) as part of a mystery play called *The Pageant of the Shearmen and Tailors*. My arrangement is in three sections and the following studies go through the basics for each part. Note the **Tierce de Picardy** (Picardy Third) a G major chord as the end of each verse. This brightens the mood from minor to major at the end of a piece of music or musical phrase, a device that was very common in this period.

*) Coventry, a large town (now city) in the West Midlands of England and an important center of the cloth trade in the Middle Ages, hence the title of the pageant.

Study 7

This study explores the fingering for the harmonies. As always, there are alternatives, so do some experimenting for yourself; for instance, I use my 2nd finger for the 3-string barre in measure 4.

▶ TRACK 66

CT

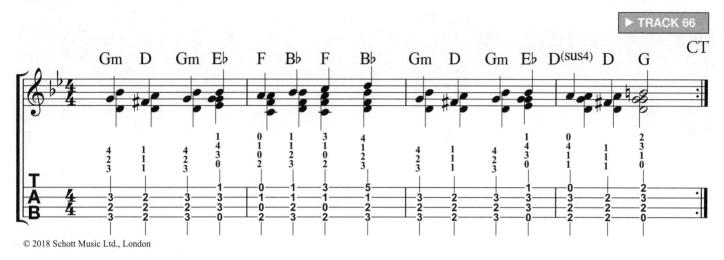

Study 8

From measure 22 in the *Coventry Carol* I use harmonies in thirds on the 2nd and 4th strings. Try my fingering first and then experiment with others you can find.

▶ TRACK 67

CT

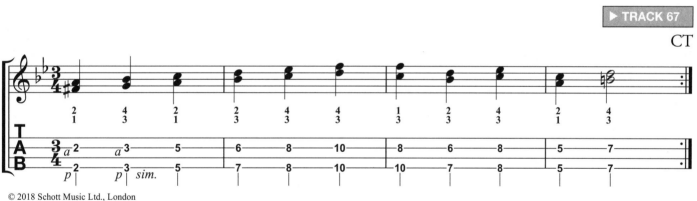

Study 9

Further work on thirds:

▶ TRACK 68

CT

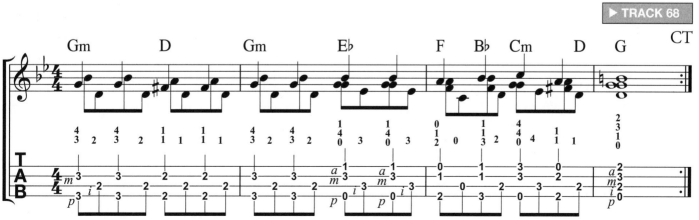

Coventry Carol

▶ TRACK 69

(Lully, Lullay)

English Traditional
Arr. Colin Tribe

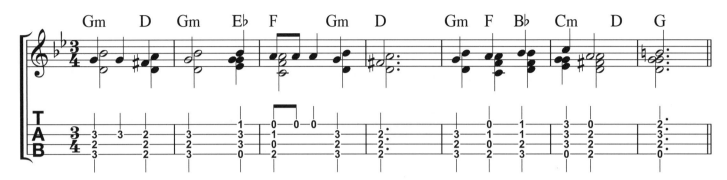

To Coda

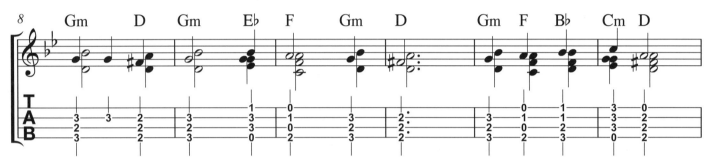

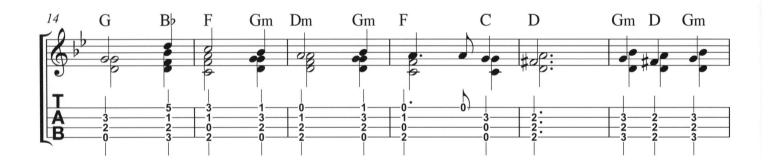

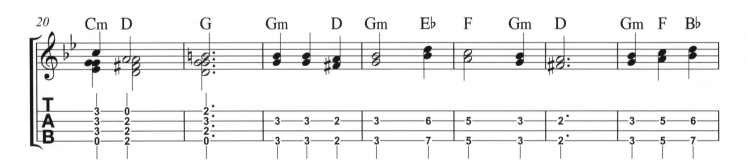

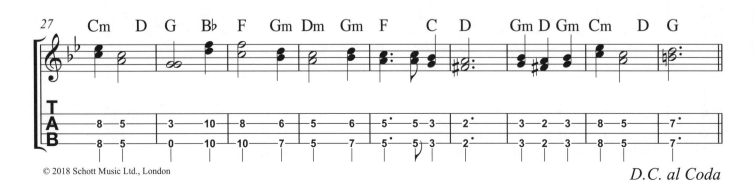

D.C. al Coda

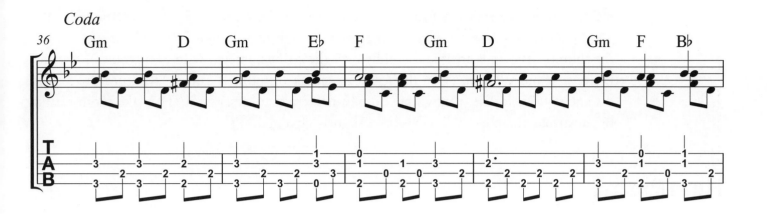

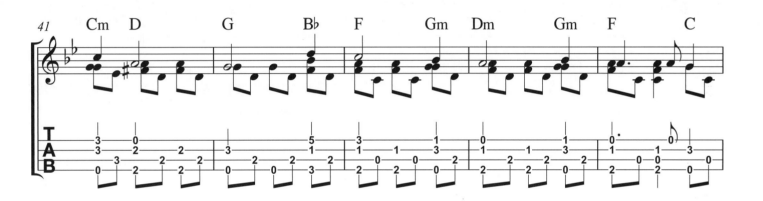

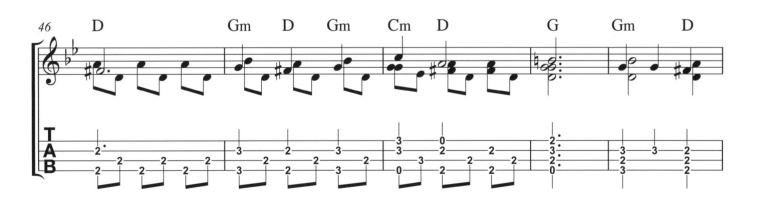

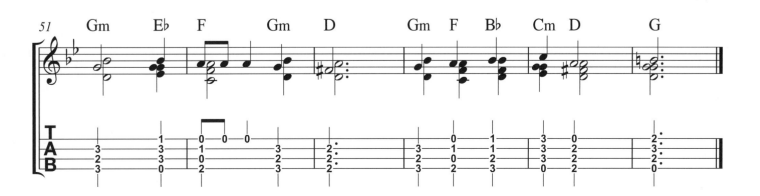

I Love Music 8

Melody with alternating strings accompaniment including a Nail Brush stroke

The Nail Brush stroke uses all four fingers of the right hand ***i m a l*** (***l*** = little finger) but not the thumb. The nails are swept rapidly over the strings; I begin with ***i*** but you can try with the reverse order ***l a m i***. In flamenco guitar playing this is called a **Rasgueado** - but in distancing the ukulele from guitar I use brush stroke to describe it. To make room for the brush stroke, the melody line has been slightly changed.

I Love Music 8

▶ TRACK 70

Arr. CT

I Love Music 9

Melody played at 5th position using barre

A strong 1st finger is needed here as it will play all the 5th fret notes. In measures 7 and 8 lift the finger to allow the open C string to play as you still hold the 5 on the G string.

Use any right-hand fingering, strummed or plucked.

I Love Music 9

▶ TRACK 71

Arr. CT

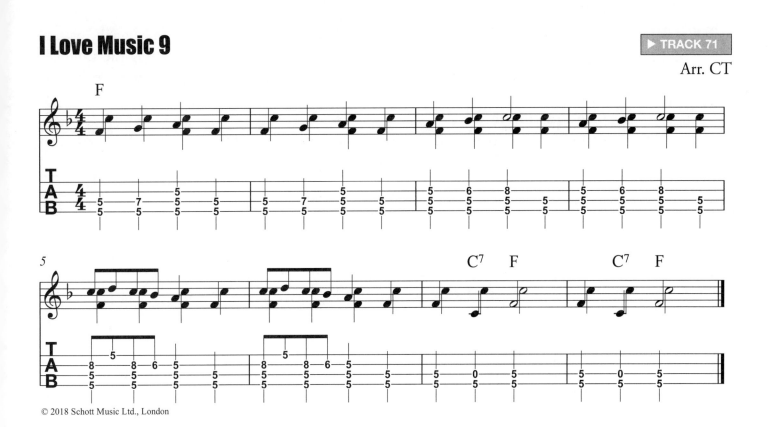

Chapter 9
Playing in the key of D minor

Let's start with some scales and chord shapes.

Study 1

Minor scales come in three different forms: Natural, Harmonic and Melodic. The natural minor scale follows the notes of the relative major (F in this case), sharing the same key signature but starting on D. Notice that the arpeggios and chords are identical for each scale.

(a) Natural minor

Play this in 1st position using open strings and work on the stretch from 3rd to 5th fret.

▶ TRACK 72

CT

(b) Harmonic minor

Note the left hand position changes, the 1st finger is at the fret marked with Roman numerals.

▶ TRACK 73

CT

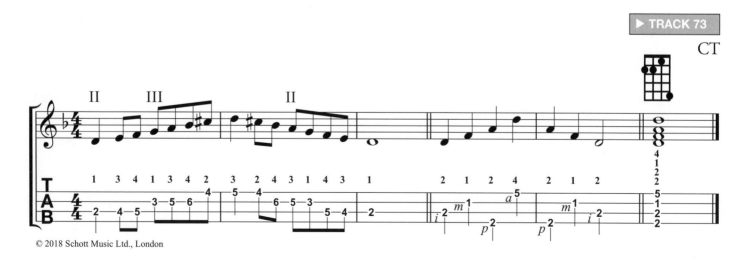

(c) Melodic minor

The 3rd finger shifts along the A string in the melodic minor between measures 1 and 2.
Notice that there are different notes when ascending and when descending.

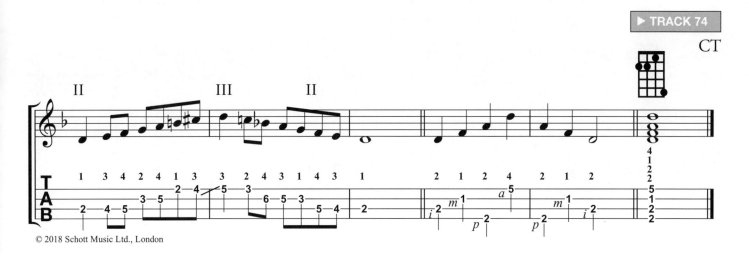

Study 2

The D minor chords in Bach's *Minuet* show some of the basic shapes for minor chords.
Experiment with double stopping to play the 2nd fret notes which should make the stretch
to D on the A string 5th fret easier.

The chord **7 5 5 8** needs a barre for the E and C strings. The triplet in measure 3 should help
you to concentrate on hearing the individual notes rather than just the chord. Note the
move of the 4th finger in this study. Use ***p i m a*** in the right hand.

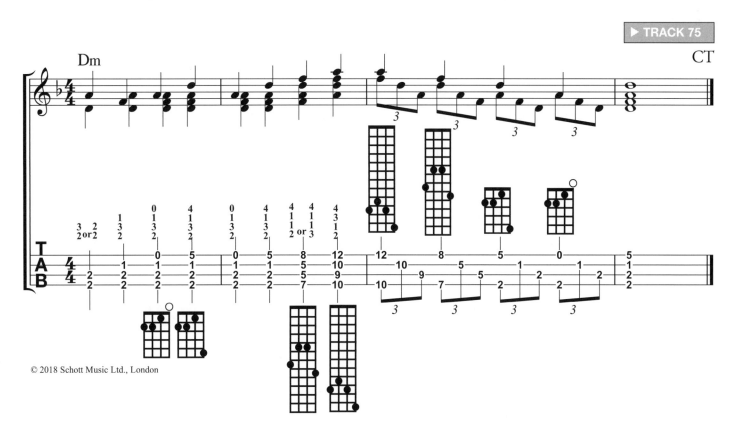

Study 3

Major chord shapes are shown through the F major chords in Bach's *Minuet* in a similar way to the minor chords in Study 2. I have also shown the fingering **0 10 10 10** for the G minor chord from the *Minuet* together with some variants of C7 to complete a "turn around" passage that is the form of the study.

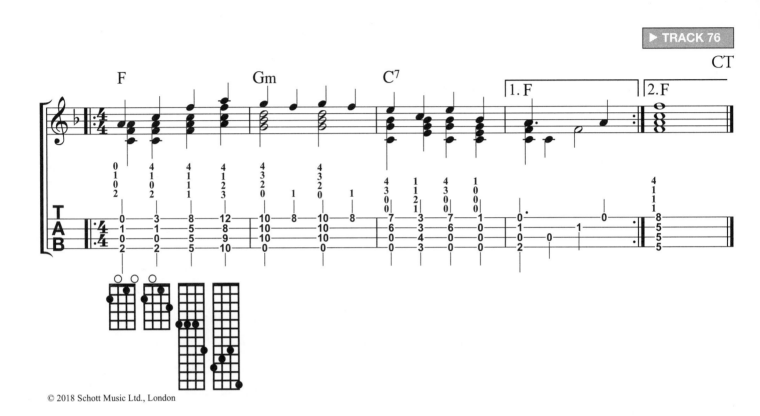

Now for two pieces by those Classical music giants, Bach and Beethoven.

The Bach *Minuet* includes two versions in one.

This shows how arrangements can be adapted by a player to suit their present skills whilst keeping the essentials of the full arrangement, which may have too many difficult fingerings to cope with at this stage. The full arrangement – which has fuller harmonies – will be worth coming back to later when you have more experience.

The top line is Version 1, the easier one to play; the bottom line is Version 2 and is notated on the central staff.

One way to approach this is to play Version 2 (V2) when you can, but use the 1st Version (V1) alternatives when you can't!

Study 4 shows the opening two measures to illustrate this:

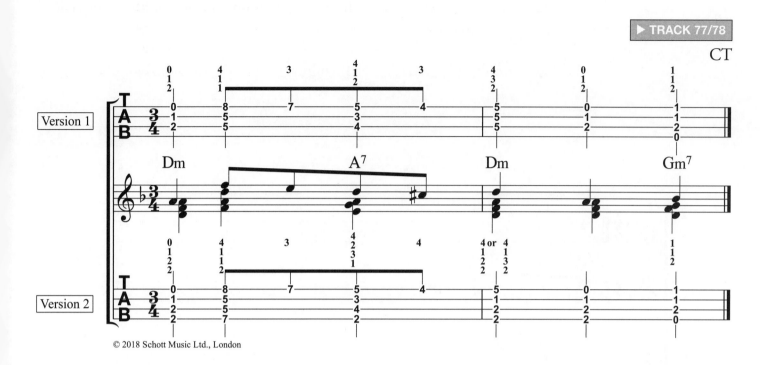

© 2018 Schott Music Ltd., London

The differences beat by beat

Measure 1

Beat 1: V1 unison A on G string left out.

Beat 2: V1 D on G string left out avoiding tricky barre and reach.

Beat 3: V1 fingers shaped like a standard G7 chord at the 4th fret but adds on the 4th finger to give the note D. Version 2 has the 4th finger working both the 5th and 4th frets.

Measure 2

Beat 1: V1 slide the 2nd finger along the C string and then reassemble the other fingers to form a 3-finger barre. V2 has the stretch to the D at the 5th fret so I use a double stop with finger 2, but it is possible to use finger 3 in this shape.

Beat 2: V1 slide finger 2 down again to fret 2 for a repeat of the opening chord. V2 lift the 4th finger.

Beat 3: V1 and V2 are identical; try to double stop with 1st finger.

Study 5

This is all about 4th finger flexibility and chromatics whilst holding other fingers in a chord shape; for this I have kept to V1 and V2 format.

Note the double stop to get the B♭ on fret 1 whilst still firmly holding the F on the E string.

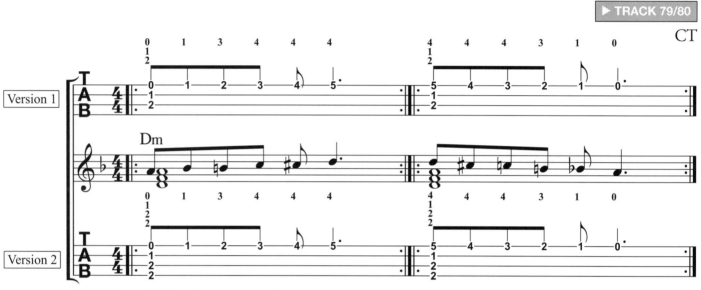

Minuet

in D minor

▶ TRACK 81

Johann Sebastian Bach (1685–1750)
Arr. Colin Tribe

I have taken many liberties in transforming Beethoven's well-known piano piece *Für Elise* into the Hackney-styled *Fürry Reggae* that I originally composed as an arrangement for Steel Band when I was teaching music in Hackney in the 1980s.*)

In this arrangement the piece highlights:

• the rhythmic chord accompaniment that is possible in a fingerstyle piece.

• the fun that can be had with the A7 chord.

• the move from Swing to straight rhythm (and back again!). In the section from measure 20 use *p i m a* plucks for the straight eights (imagine a woodpecker rhythmically pecking a tree) before returning to the Swing feel in measure 36.

---

*) Hackney is an inner-London borough in the UK celebrated for its cultural diversity.

Study 6

The rhythmic motif is shown here. Sometimes a melody line will interrupt the flow; in general the melody is the more important element so it is given prominence, although I would blur the distinction in strummed choruses for repeats as a variation from the original.

A useful principle is to use a *p i m a* pluck on the first beat of a measure, giving that first beat definition: try it in this study. Although I have shown the down strokes as being played with *i,* that is a matter of taste. You can use any combination of finger nails for these important little rhythmic brush stroke figures. The thumbnail will naturally play the up strokes.

If you look at the staff notation you will notice some anomalies:

• the whole note F at the start is recycled as part of the strummed chord.

• where a chord includes unison notes I have omitted them for clarity.

• in measures 2 and 4 your strum could include the open A string as that note is already being heard – so strumming it in error is not a problem and makes it easier to do!

▶ TRACK 82

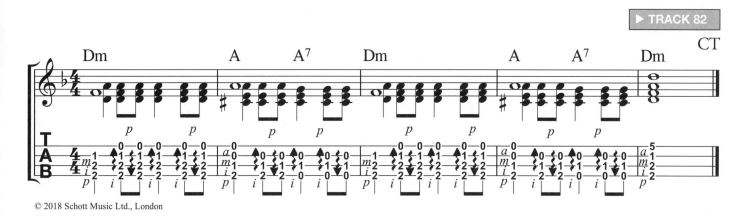

Study 7

A7 is a great chord to play on the ukulele as it uses three of the open strings A-E-G (Am7/C6 is even better as it is just the 4 open strings!). Beethoven uses octave figures in his piano piece, but the ukulele simply can't do many of those so we go up the arpeggio of A7 using octaves on the 1st and 3rd strings whilst the G and E ring open. To help you finger this I have worked it into this study which also has a note from the diminished chord to spice it up!

▶ TRACK 83

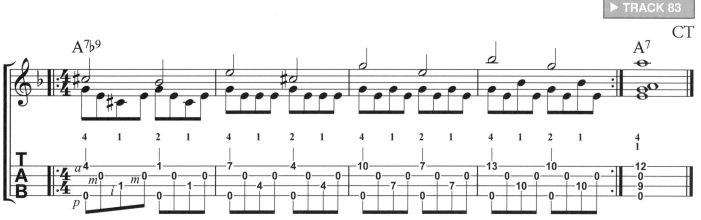

Fürry Reggae

▶ TRACK 84

Ludwig van Beethoven (1770–1827)
Freely adapted and arranged by Colin Tribe

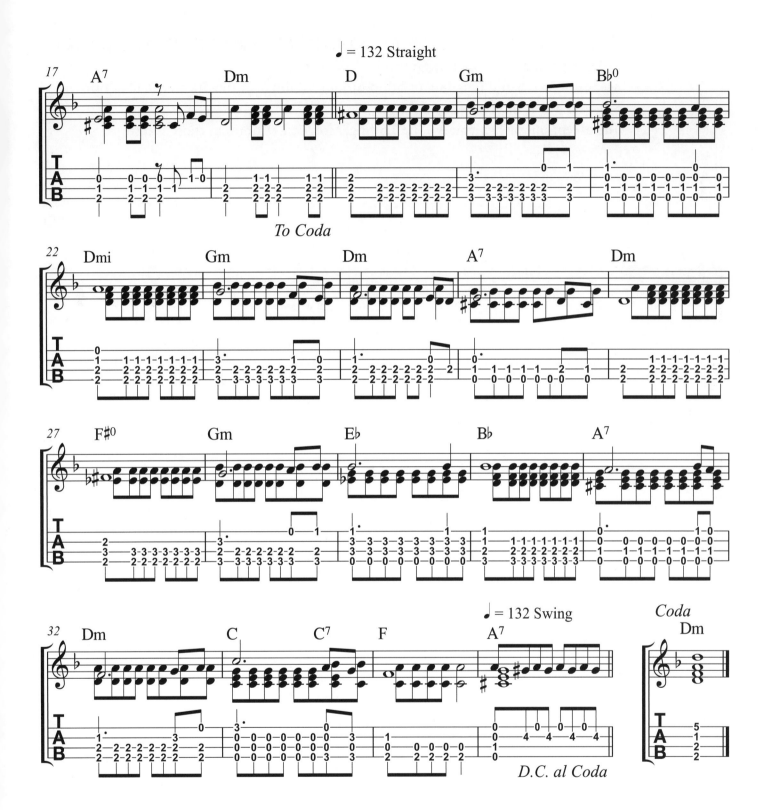

I Love Music 10

Melody on one string E (except for two notes) with open C drone accompaniment

Measures 1 and 2 in 1st position (finger 1 on fret 1)
Measures 3, 4, 5 and 6 mainly in 5th position: 1st finger at the 5th fret, 2nd at 6th, 3rd at 8th, and 4th at the 10th fret
The exception is when you use the 1st finger for 1st fret notes in those measures.

▶ TRACK 85

Arr. CT

I Love Music 11

Melody below high F

Use a barre at the 5th fret with 1st finger, the 4th finger is anchored on the 8th fret to give the F; frets 6 and 7 are played with the 2nd and 3rd fingers. Right hand: one way is to pluck the high F with *a* and use *p* for all the other notes, but as always experiment with other possibilities to suit you.

▶ TRACK 86

Arr. CT

Chapter 10
Playing in the key of E minor

Study 1

This study uses *p i m a* arpeggios to explore some different ways to play E minor and its dominant 7th B7.

▶ TRACK 87

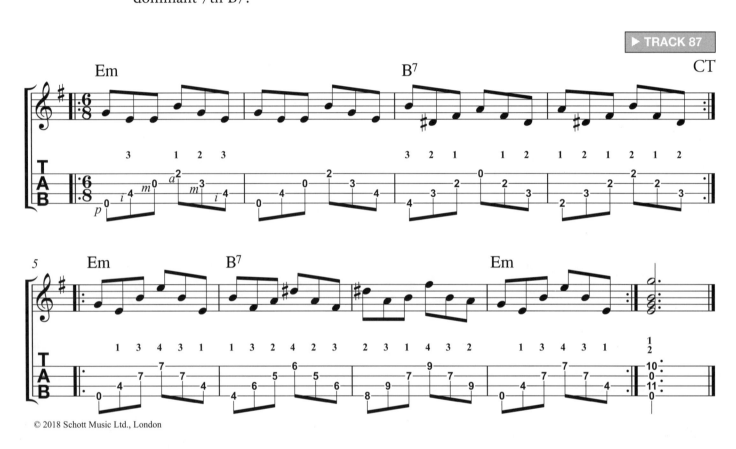

Study 2

Silence! This study shows different ways of muting and stopping strings sounding in staccato passages and during rests.

Measures 1, 2 and 3 use "FM" to stand for Finger Mute when, after the 8th note melody note, the 4th finger comes down lightly to touch all the strings (and especially the open ones) to stop them vibrating.

Measure 4 has no open strings, so the technique is to lift the left-hand fingers fractionally to stop the sound before bringing them back down for the chord to sound again.

Measure 5 uses both techniques simultaneously with the 3rd finger being the one to stop the G string vibrating whilst the lift does the other three strings.

▶ TRACK 88

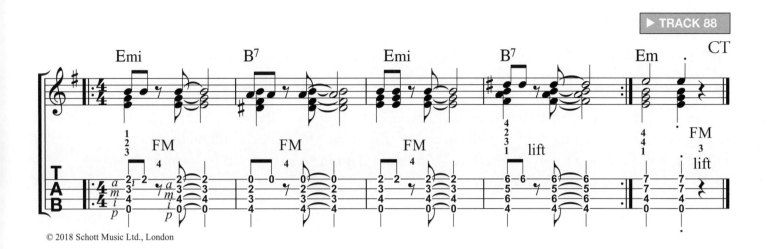

Study 3

Whilst exploring these muting techniques, have some fun with Mendelssohn's *Wedding March* (*Rock Around the Clock* starts in a similar fashion).

Measure 1: C string open – 1st finger mutes G while the 4th finger mutes E and A;
Measure 2: C and E strings open – 1st finger mutes G while the 4th finger mutes A;
Measure 3: C, E and G open – 4th finger mutes A;
Measure 4: No muting!

The right hand uses *i* for down strokes and *p* for up which gives a slightly unusual but good hesitant feel to the 1st beat of each measure. End with a *p i m a* stroke.

▶ TRACK 89

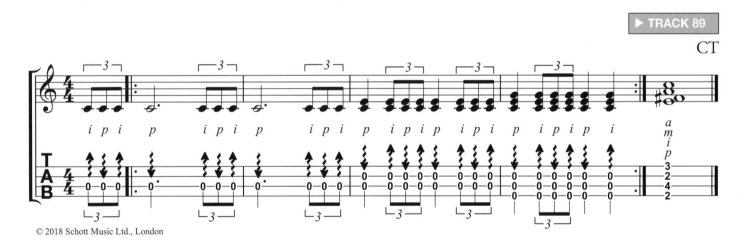

Study 4

Here are some useful double stopping ideas with the 2nd finger as you hold the chords and use the sustained harmony to accompany the melody.

In measure 2 the 2nd finger is playing D♯ on C string 3rd fret; try to collapse the joint so as to play G on the 2nd string 3rd fret with the pad of that finger whilst the tip still holds the D♯. You could try the same idea in measure 4, 2nd note C on the A string, but that is more tricky so 3 is a good alternative as shown.

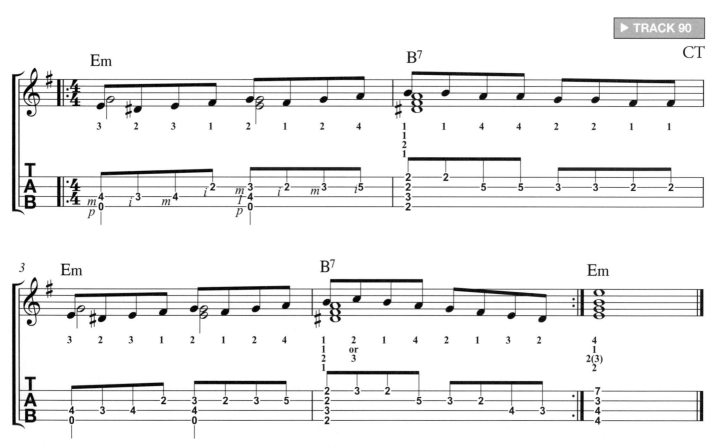

Joshua Fought the Battle of Jericho

► TRACK 91

African-American Traditional
Arr. Colin Tribe

D.S. al Coda

Study 5

Dimished chords are made up of groups of minor 3rds piled on top of each other. They repeat at three-fret intervals, the same shape giving the same four notes but in different orders.

In this study I use the chord name based on the note on the G string, but any of the four notes could be used. Measures 1, 2 and 3 each contain the same notes for each chord in the measure, but measures 4 and 5 are a chromatic series.

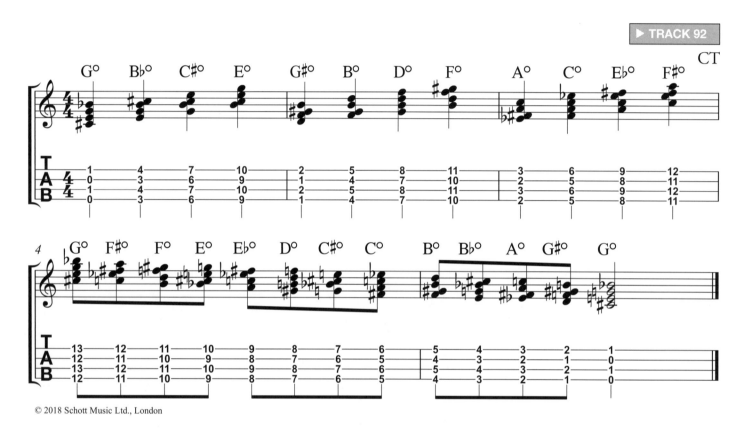

Study 6

This study focuses on slurs which can be acheived by hammer-ons, pull-offs and slides. Notice that in measure 3 the first four notes are played by plucking the string just once – then slide down, then up and finally hammer-on. Gradually you will be able to get the sound to carry on through.

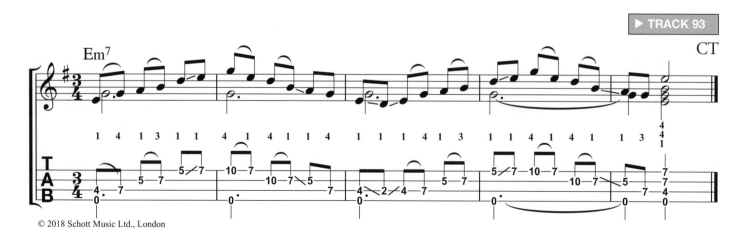

Study 7

Natural harmonics are produced when a vibrating string is touched – but not stopped – at the 12th, 5th or 7th frets. The touch is made over the fret itself and some practice is needed to get the ringing sound you want. I can feel the string bounce under my finger and actually use the pad of my 3rd finger since that fleshy part seems more suited to producing the sound than others, but as always feel free to experiment and find what works best for you.

The resulting notes can be seen in the chart below which leads into an arrangement of *When the Saints Go Marching In* in the key of G.

▶ TRACK 94
CT

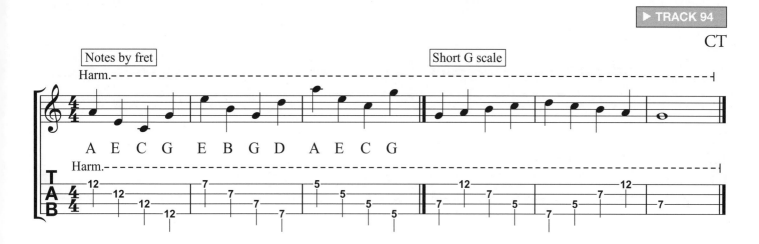

When the Saints Go Marching In

▶ TRACK 95

African-American Traditional
Arr. Colin Tribe

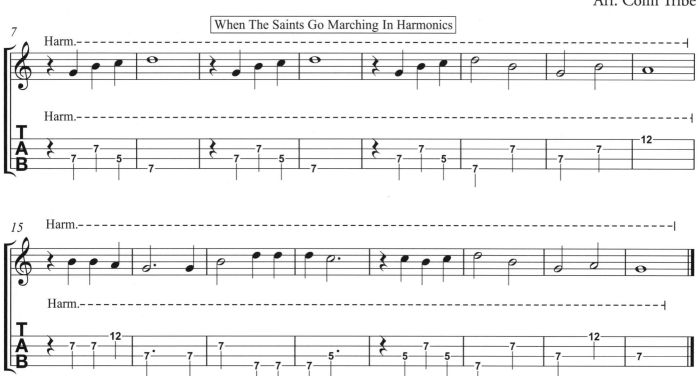

Study 8

With the right hand fluent in combinations of *p i m a* strokes you can play either triplets or sixteenth note passages with a small adjustment. Both patterns are used in *Perpetually Diminishing*. Although the triplets have been written as 6/8 and the sixteenths are played a lot faster in the piece, it makes for a good study as the two patterns are played in sequence.

Notice how, in measure 14 of *Perpetually Diminishing*, the open A allows time to move the hand up to play the 11th and12th fret notes, then return back to the 1st position when the next open A is played.

Perpetually Diminishing

▶ TRACK 97

Colin Tribe

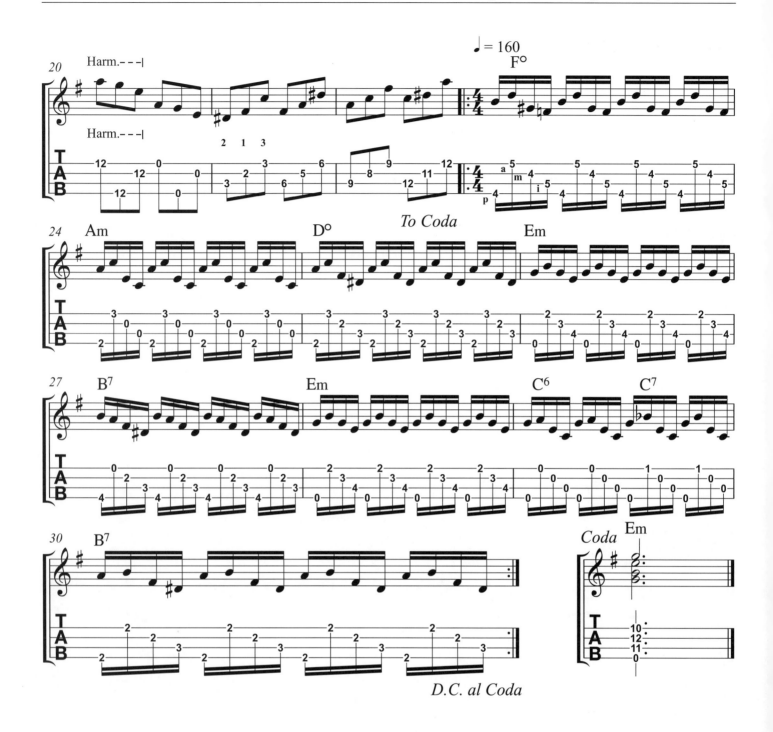

To Coda

D.C. al Coda

I Love Music 12

Melody in thirds over C

Use *p i m* to pluck or roll this chord melody version using only three strings.

▶ TRACK 98

CT

I Love Music 13

Melody over C in triplets – the melody is the 3rd note of each triplet

The same chords as in *I Love Music* 12; use *p i m* except in measures 5 and 6 which start *p i p, p i p.*

▶ TRACK 99

Arr. CT

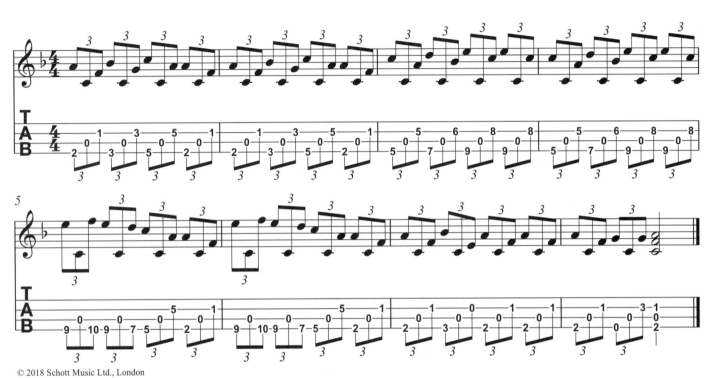

Chapter 11
Playing in the key of D major

Study 1

The scale of D major is an excellent model from which to learn the fingering pattern for many major scales. The arpeggio pattern in measure 4 I have called "impact" as it starts with the right hand finger order *i m p a* which generally gives the notes in ascending sound order.

▶ TRACK 100

© 2018 Schott Music Ltd., London

Study 2

Here is a chord study based on the triads formed by the scale. In the ascending form I have used D major but descending it goes into B minor.

▶ TRACK 101

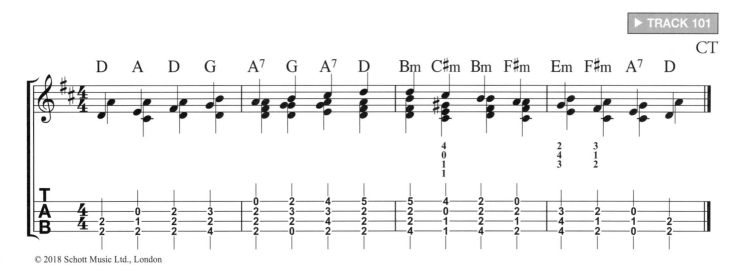

© 2018 Schott Music Ltd., London

Play *Ave Verum Corpus* with as much sustain to the chords as possible. The left-hand fingering may not always seem the simplest way to play, but it will allow notes to continue ringing.

The right hand often uses slow *p i m a* rolls, but also has some brush strokes on the chord rhythmic repetitions as in measure 7, beats 2 and 3.

Ave Verum Corpus

(K618)

Wolfgang Amadeus Mozart (1756–1795)
Arr. Colin Tribe

▶ TRACK 102

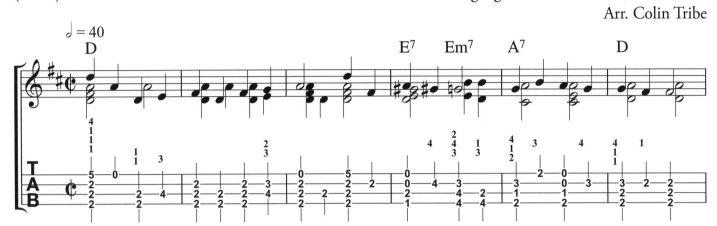

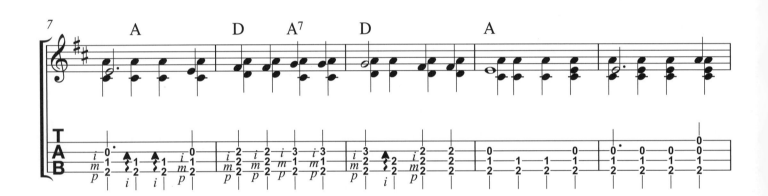

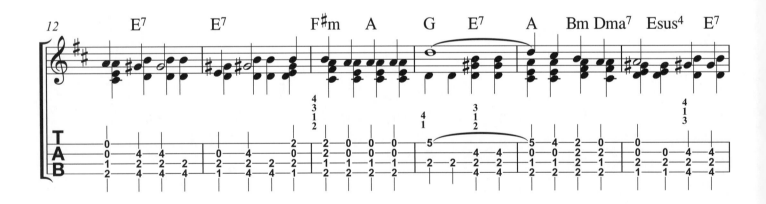

Study 3

La Paloma uses just two chords, tonic D and dominant A7. This study interweaves versions of both chords.

▶ TRACK 103

CT

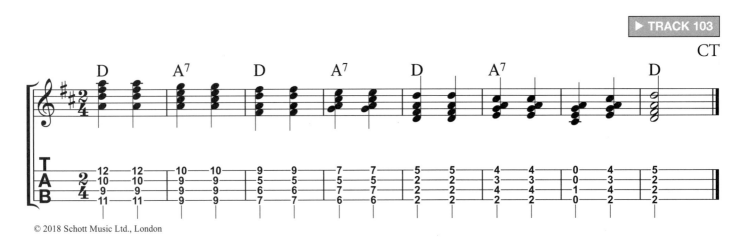

Study 4

The D chord often consists of the **2 2 2 X** core with other notes on the A string. Some of the possibilities are shown here, plus an alternative to **2 2 2 7** if your stretch doesn't quite make it.

▶ TRACK 104

CT

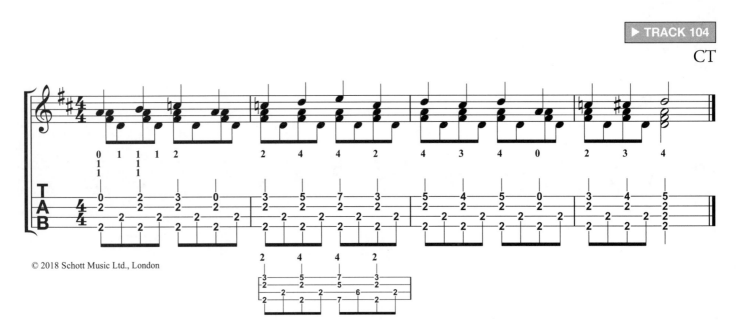

Study 5

In *La Paloma*, from measure 37, the tune is harmonised in 3rds and 6ths; this study explores these intervals.

▶ TRACK 105

CT

La Paloma

(The Dove)

▶ TRACK 106

Sebastián Iradier (1809–1865)
Arr. Colin Tribe

D.C. al Fine

I Love Music 14

Melody over C in triplets; the melody note is the first in each triplet

Use *m i p* except in measures 5 and 6 which start *p i p, p i p*

▶ TRACK 107

CT

Chapter 12
Playing in the key of A major

The note A has a unique property on the Ukulele – you can play it on all four strings at the same time with a bit of a stretch! The shape is **2 9 5 0,** fingers 1, 4, 2; the 3rd finger doesn't touch the G string – even though it looks close to it!

Fig. 12

Study 1

This study uses all the notes; the **Z** symbol indicates a fast nail brush stroke on the second eighth note of each measure. Three of the four A's in the first chord are replaced in turn by G, E and C♭ until you have the chord of A7 which is the dominant 7th of D major.

▶ TRACK 108

CT

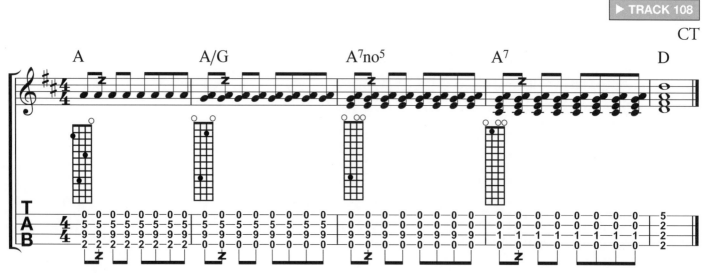

Study 2

The repeat in *My Bonnie Lies Over the Ocean* has the accompaniment in triplets, as in this study which shows the three main chords in A major in different inversions.

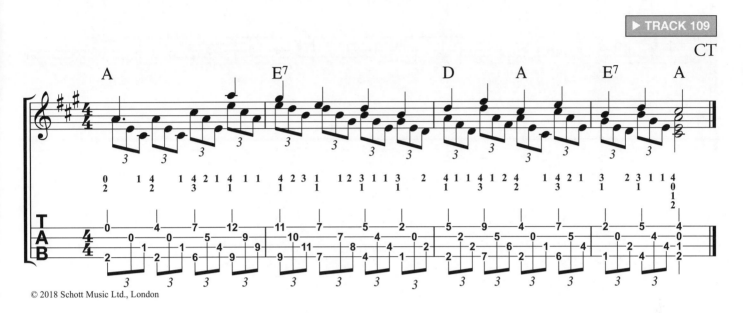

Some of the tied notes in *My Bonnie Lies Over the Ocean*, such as in measure 36, are not actually possible but they indicate a feeling of smoothness.

My Bonnie Lies Over the Ocean

▶ TRACK 110

Scottish Traditional
Arr. Colin Tribe

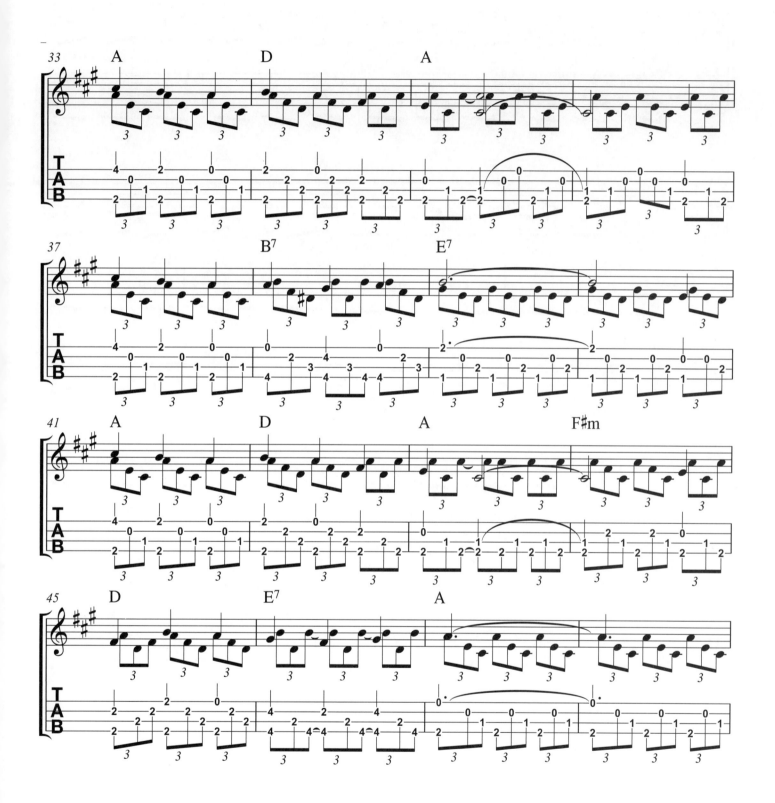

Study 3

The ability to play barre chords with all four fingers will come in useful when quick changes are needed; for example, try out the 3rd finger barre in the 1st measure of *All Things Bright and Beautiful*:

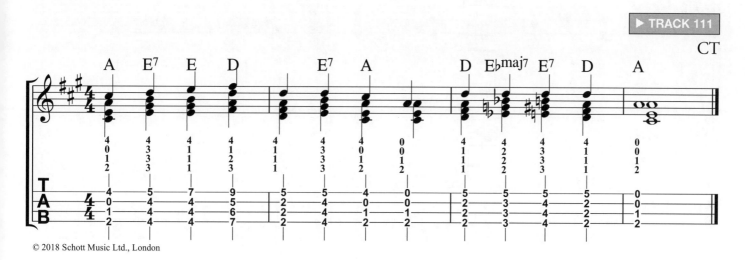

All Things Bright and Beautiful

(Melody *Royal Oak*)

▶ TRACK 112

English Traditional
Arr. Colin Tribe

Fine

D.C. al Fine

Here are two studies highlighting elements of *The Saltash Blues* *)

Study 4

This study focuses on the combination of the 3rd and 4th strings in harmony to produce an interval of a sixth; I use it get to the chord which is then played as an arpeggio over all four strings. When approaching the E7 chord the anatomy of the ukulele dictates a move to 1st and 2nd strings in thirds to avoid an awkward 13th fret note on the G string.

▶ TRACK 113

CT

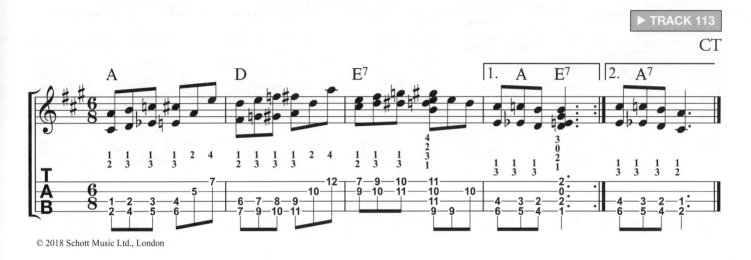

Study 5

Power chords on the guitar (using the 1st and 5th degrees of the scale without the 3rd), translate well to the ukulele.

▶ TRACK 114

CT

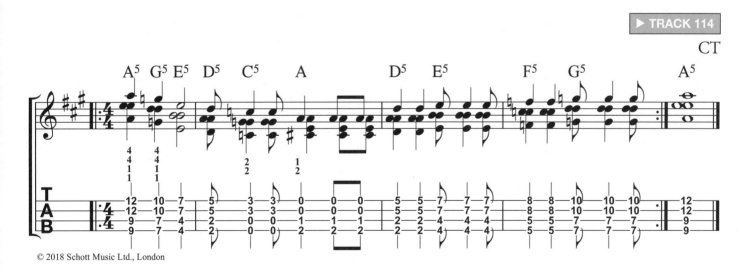

*) Saltash, a town in the southeast of Cornwall on the banks of the River Tamar

Saltash Blues

▶ TRACK 115

Colin Tribe

I Love Music 15

Melody in thirds over C in triplets

Use *p* and *m*, *i*, *p* and *m*.

▶ TRACK 116

Arr. CT

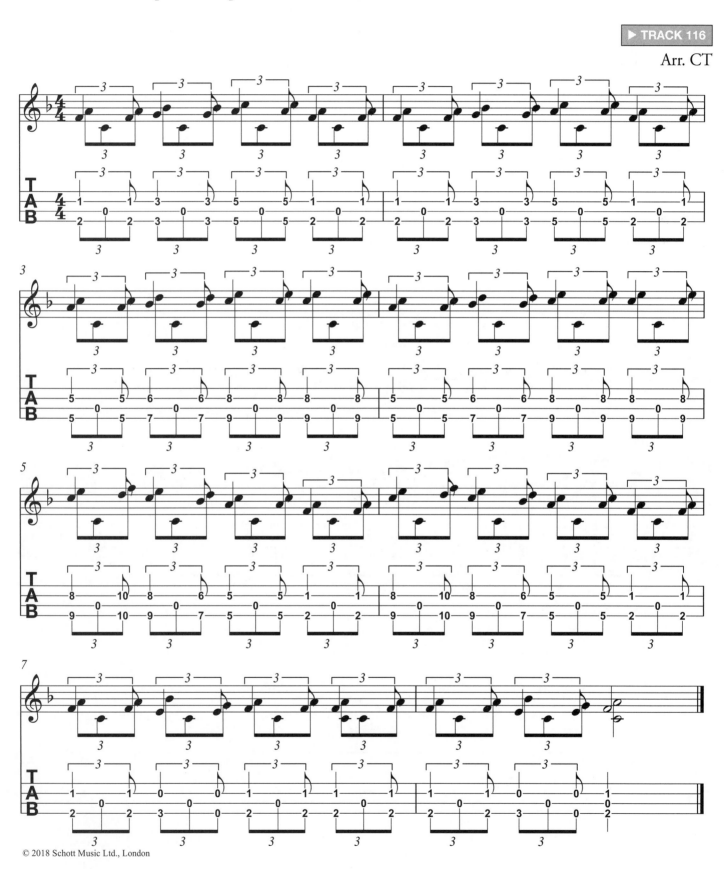

Chapter 13
Chromatics

Study 1: Descending

Use the same fingers as the respective frets. When you have learned the pattern, continue repeating the four measure sections up the fretboard till you reach the 12th fret with the 4th finger; you will now be playing the A chromatic scale, descending.

▶ TRACK 117

CT

Study 2: Ascending

As in Study 1, use the same fingers as the respective frets. When you have learned the pattern continue up the fretboard till you reach the 12th fret with the 4th finger; you will now be playing the A chromatic scale, ascending.

▶ TRACK 118

CT

The Chromatic Rag

▶ TRACK 119

CT

To Coda

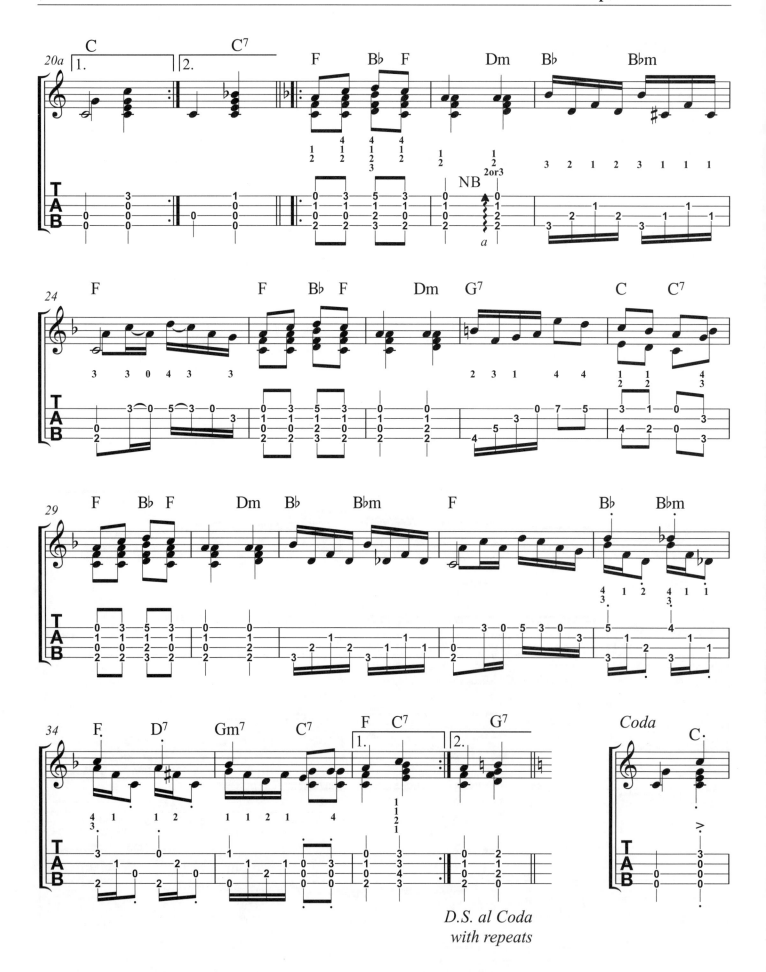

D.S. al Coda
with repeats

The Strangely-Timed Chromatic Blues

▶ TRACK 120

12-Bar Blues in C

CT

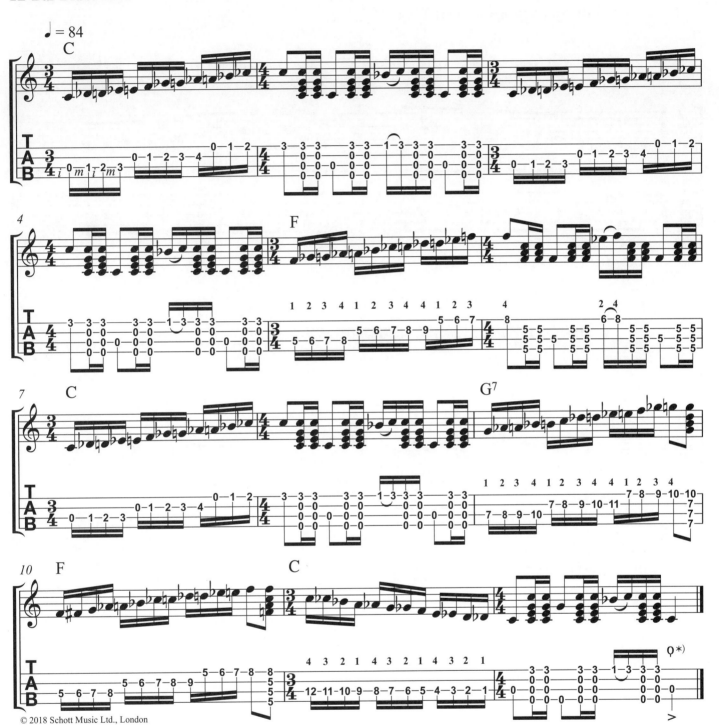

© 2018 Schott Music Ltd., London

---

*) ϙ = pluck with the C string with *p* & *i*, gripping it so the string snaps against the frets with a musical twang!

Study 3: Chromatic scale on one string

Repeat this study on the other three strings; experiment with different right-hand fingerings after mastering *i m* alternating.

▶ TRACK 121

CT

© 2018 Schott Music Ltd., London

Study 4: Contrary motion chromatic scale

▶ TRACK 122

CT

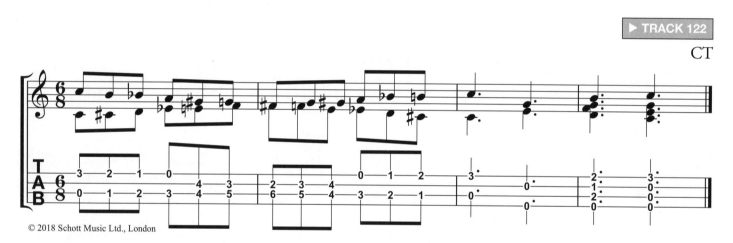

© 2018 Schott Music Ltd., London

I Love Music 16

Melody with tremolo

Use right-hand pattern *p a m i*

▶ TRACK 123

CT

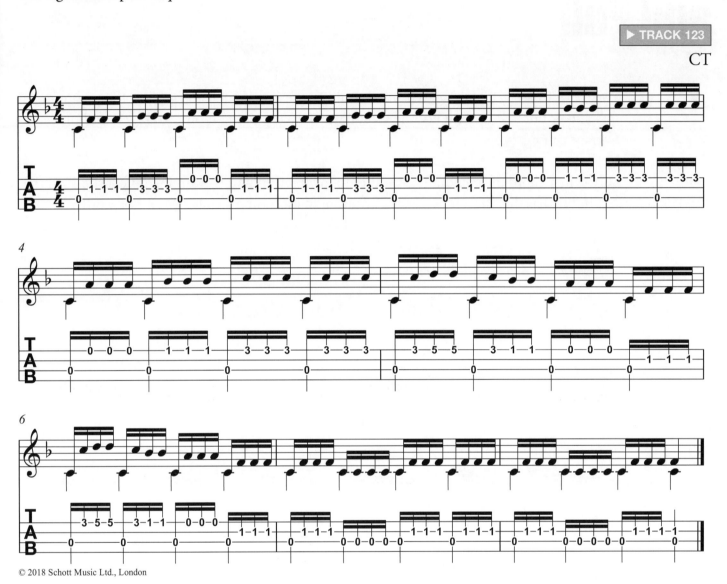

Chapter 14
Using Arpeggios and Hammer and Pull

Arpeggios are generally played in ascending note order – left to right on the piano for instance – but that is often not the most natural way of doing it on the ukulele with its re-entrant tuning.

The first chord in ascending note order following the G-C-E-A tuning is G at the 10th fret. Study 1 has the final chord in each measure in ascending string-note-*p i m a* order.

Study 1

▶ TRACK 124

CT

Study 2

p i m a is excellent for playing arpeggios in 6/8 time as in this treatment of the opening chords of Leonard Cohen's *Hallelujah*.

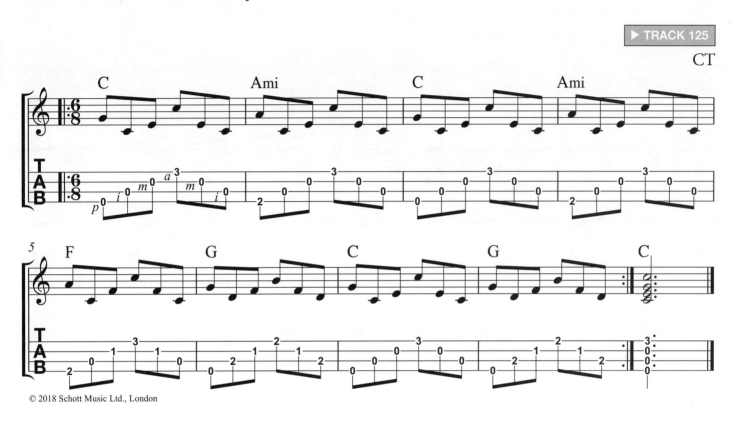

Study 3

To accommodate re-entrant tuning in standard arpeggio playing I use a right-hand pattern I have termed "***impa***ct". This study explores this important pattern.

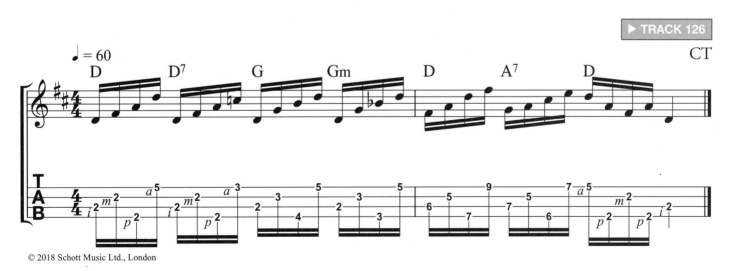

Study 4

Romanza is a traditional Spanish piece, well-known in the classical guitar repertoire, which uses open strings to provide the bass line. My ukulele adaptation takes the basic patterns but plays around with the harmonies to it make effective. This study incorporates the arpeggio pattern with some unusual chords.

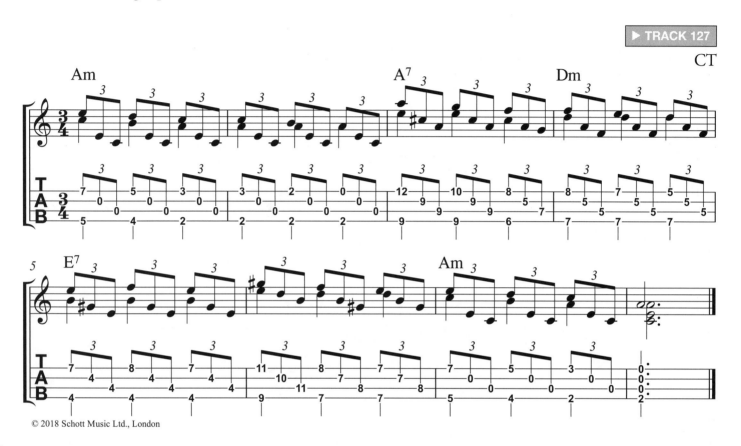

Romanza

▶ TRACK 128

Anonymous
Arr. Colin Tribe

Fine

D.C. al Fine

Study 5

The arpeggios in *Jasmine Flower* are not so difficult as they may seem and the left hand is quite easy, letting you concentrate on the right. Here are some examples where you subtly change the right-hand pattern to make sure you can identify and play the version required.

Note the performance instruction "Very Freely"; this can apply both to the tempo and tone and the addition of slides, hammer-ons and pull-offs. Some are indicated in the score but your choices should reflect your own interpretation. Listen to some other interpretations of the piece (easily available online) to help you decide how you want to play it.

Jasmine Flower

Chinese Traditional
Arr. Colin Tribe

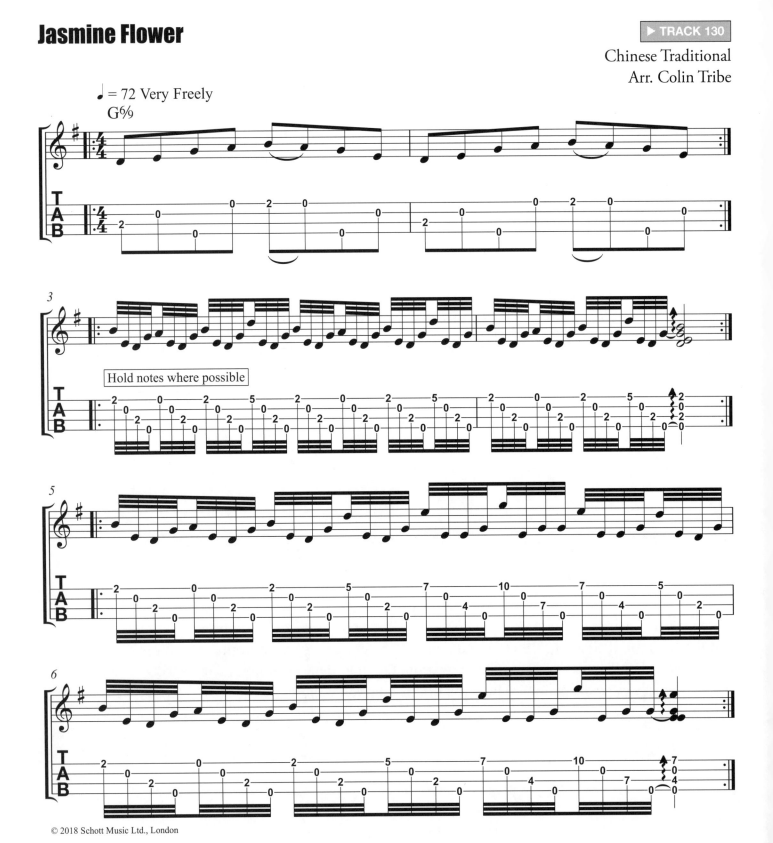

Study 6

This study rehearses an important technique from the opening measure of *Hammer & Pull*. On the first measure play a roll (a fast but separated arpeggio), but vary the stroke on the third beat with a simultaneous plucked chord.

The title *Hammer & Pull* comes from the triplets on the third beat when after the first chord is sounded the third finger hammers-on the second triplet and pulls-off again to sound the third one.

▶ TRACK 131

CT

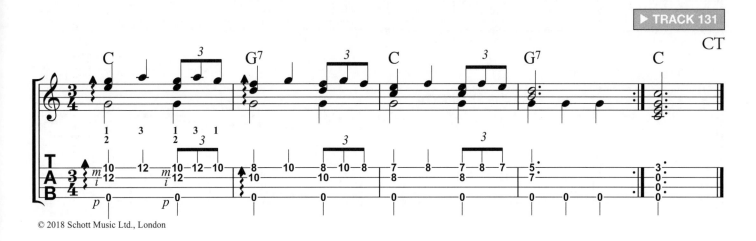

Study 7

In this study pluck the first note (called a **grace note**) and then slide the 4th finger rapidly along the string. I sometimes use the 3rd finger as a support to the 4th, gently leaning it on top to give added strength and certainty of a good contact. Use this technique in measures 20, 21 and 24 of the piece.

▶ TRACK 132

CT

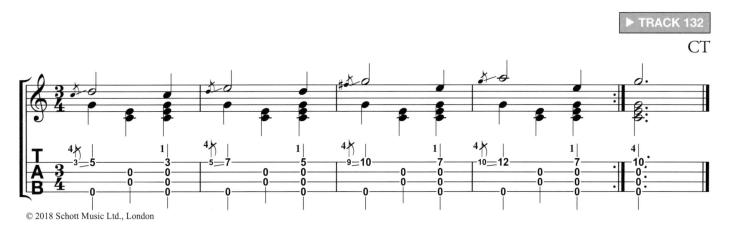

Hammer & Pull

Colin Tribe

D.C. al Coda

I Love Music 17

My final arrangement of this piece has the tune played as a **round** (or canon) in which the
melody restarts at 2-measure intervals numbered here above the staff.

Measures 1/2   : one part
Measures 3/4   : two parts
Measures 5/6   : three parts
Measures 7/8   : four parts
Measures 9/10   : three parts
Measures 11/12 : two parts
Measures 13/14 : one part

▶ TRACK 134

Arr. CT

Chapter 15
Repertoire Pieces

All My Trials

▶ TRACK 135

Caribbean Traditional
Arr. Colin Tribe

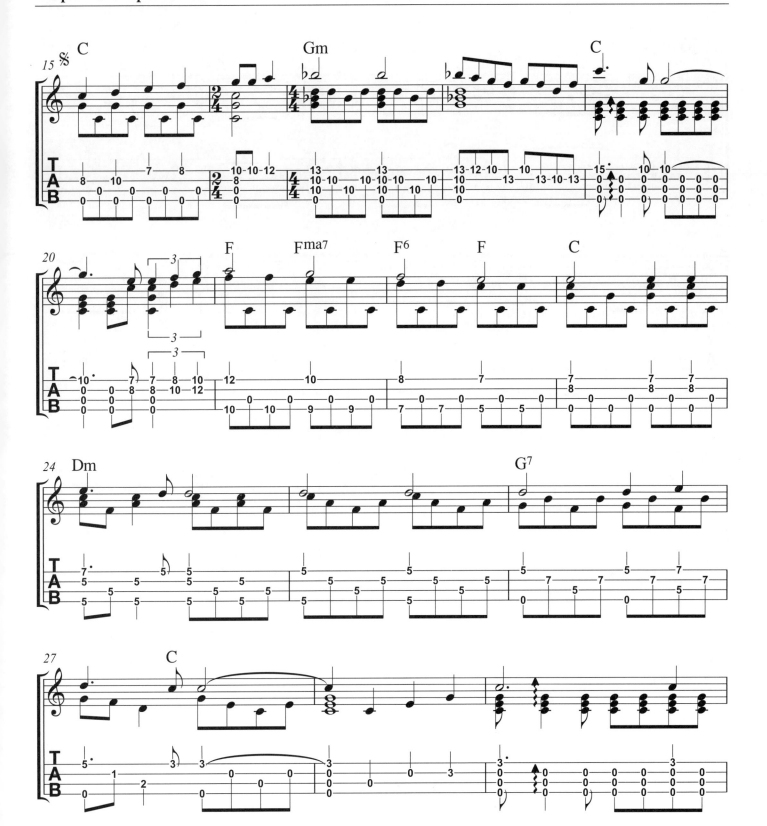

To Coda   *D.S. al Coda,*

Jupiter

(Theme from *The Planets*)

TRACK 136

Gustav Holst (1874–1934)
Arr. Colin Tribe

Swan Lake

▶ TRACK 137

(Theme from the Finale)

Pyotr Ilyich Tchaikovsky (1840–1893)
Arr. Colin Tribe

Chapter 16
Anatomy of the ukulele

The following charts and diagrams are to help you understand and remember where to find the notes – the nuts and bolts – of the ukulele. This book does not claim to be an encyclopedia, so use these as starting points to discover more about the instrument for yourself.

Note chart

At first glance this looks like one of those flight path charts shown on a plane's in-flight entertainment and information screen. I have left out sharps and flats for clarity!

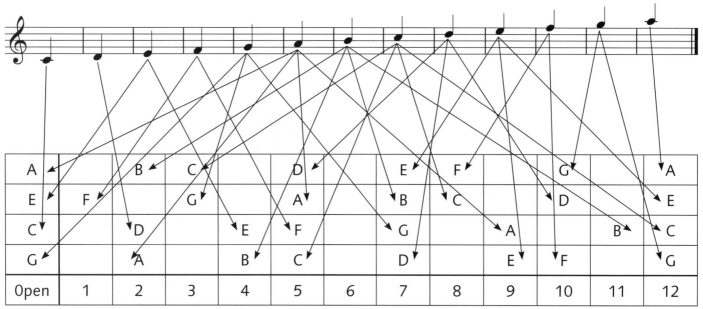

© 2018 Schott Music Ltd, London

The musical compass of a 12-fret ukulele with high G re-entrant tuning:

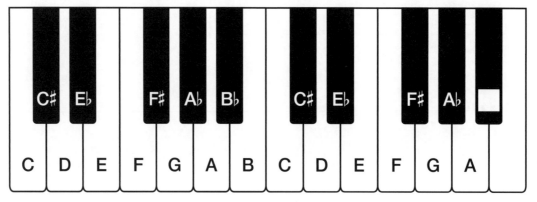

© 2018 Schott Music Ltd, London

Note finder for the ukulele

with re-entrant high G tuning

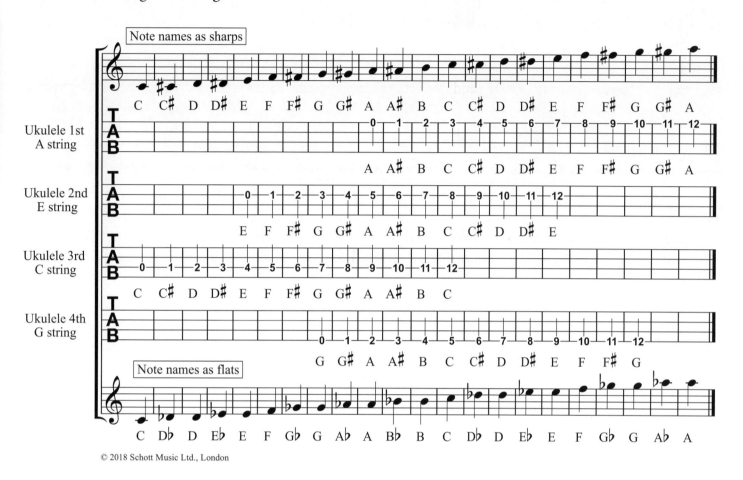

Scales

Here are the basic scale patterns shown at open and 5th positions. Use them as templates for scales in all other keys.

C major

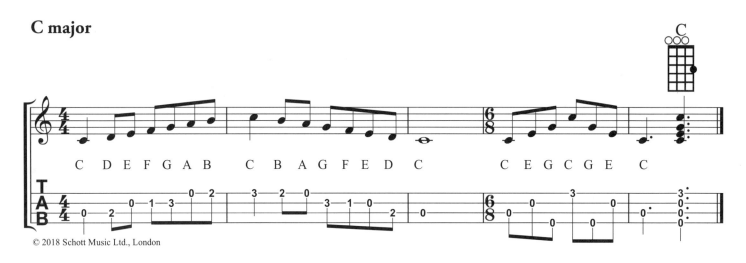

© 2018 Schott Music Ltd., London

F major

© 2018 Schott Music Ltd., London

C harmonic minor

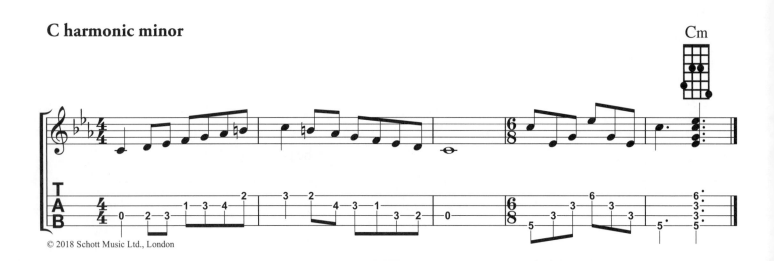

© 2018 Schott Music Ltd., London

F harmonic minor

Note the changes of position dictated by the 1st finger frets.

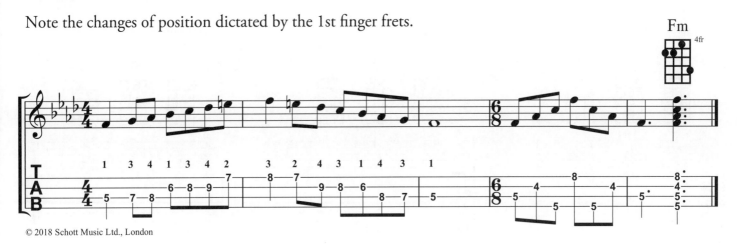

Chords

Strummers' chords usually contain three notes one of which being doubled as demonstrated in these versions of E minor:

Doubling B   **Doubling G**   **Doubling E**

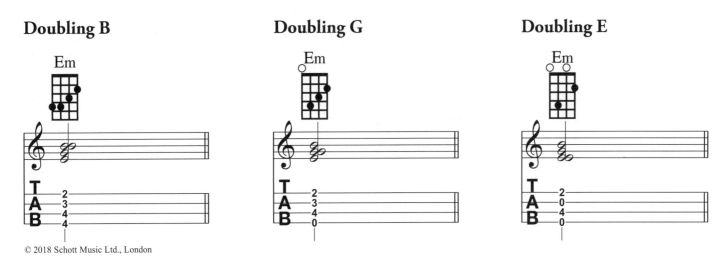

Strumming singers use their voices to carry the melody over the basic chord shapes. A fingerstyle player, however, plays the melody as notes which are parts of chords. The chords give voice to the harmony and rhythm accompanying the melody, often recycling the melody notes.

The four-part chord shapes shown below use open strings in their lowest position, but the significant feature is that they can be moved up the fingerboard to be played at any fret: the lowest numbered fret used is known as its "position".

I will show and name these moveable chords at the open, 1st and 5th positions.

Try to work out the other possibilities for each chord, referring to the 12-fret note chart to check the notes being played in each position. You will gain familiarity with them by repetition, so use them at every opportunity.

Major

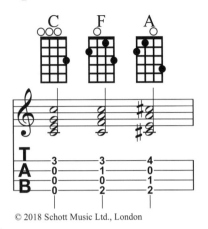

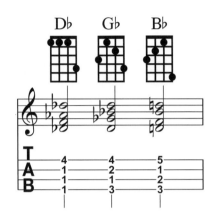

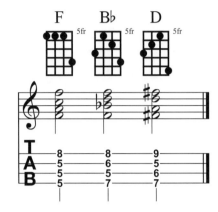

Minor

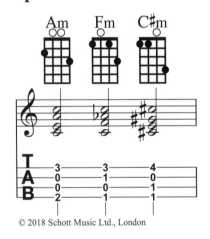

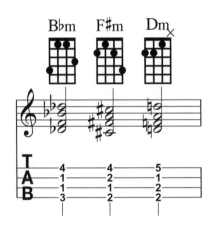

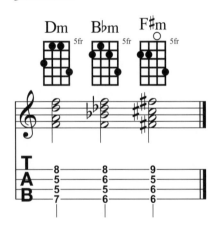

Dominant 7th

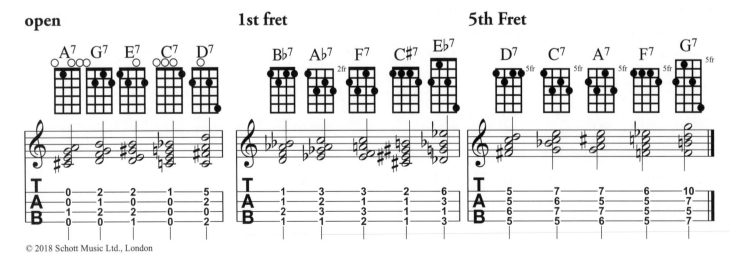

Major 7th

open   **1st fret**

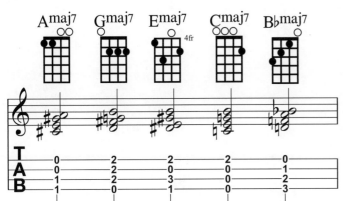

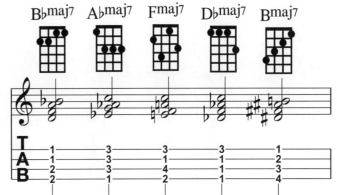

5th Fret

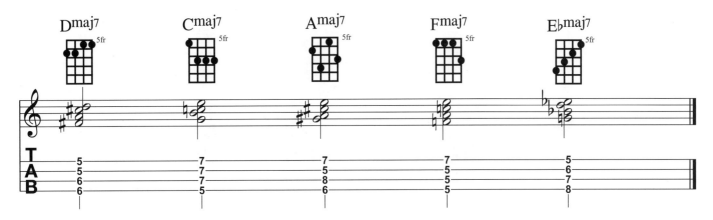

Minor 7th

open   **1st fret**   **5th Fret**

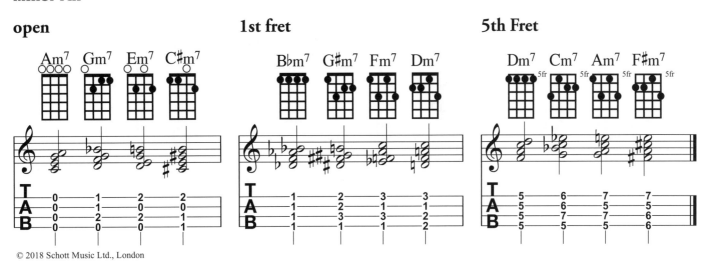

Diminished

There are four different names for each shape for diminished chords. All four notes of the chord can be that chord's name.

G° or B♭° or C♯° or E°
A♭° or B° or D° or F°
A° or C° or E♭° or F♭°

Here they are from open to 12th fret:

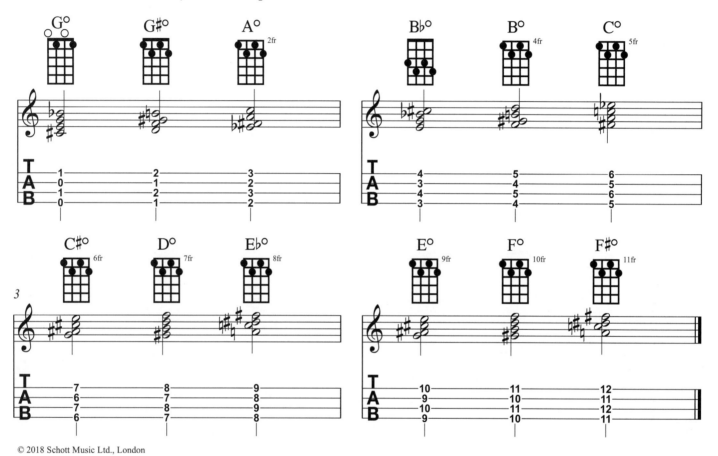

Augmented

There are three different names for each shape for augmented chords. All three notes of the chord can be that chord's name.

G⁺ or B⁺ or Eb⁺
Ab⁺ or C+ or E⁺
A⁺ or C##⁺ or F⁺
Bb⁺ or D⁺ or F##⁺

Here they are from open to 3rd fret:

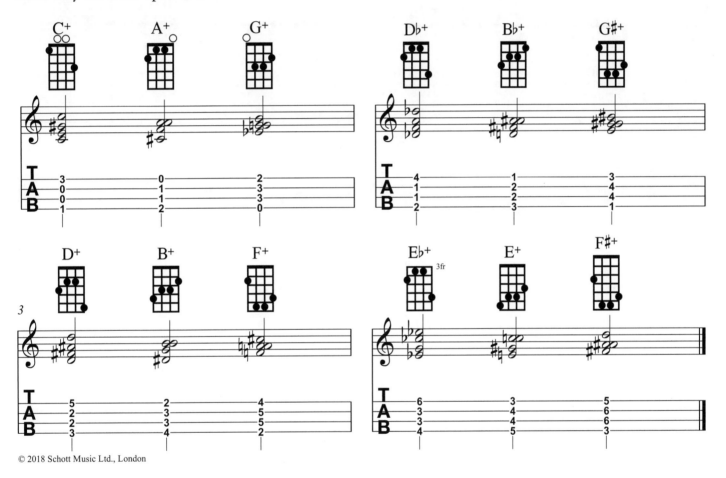

A Miscellany of chord fun!

Try these ideas for yourself and keep experimenting with your fingers to find new possibilities.

Study 1

Chord changer study, using major, minor and dominant 7th chords.

Study 2

Major 6th. This uses the same notes as a minor 7th but in context generally has a gentler demeanour! Everyone can play C6 as an open chord, but here is how it changes as it moves up the frets.

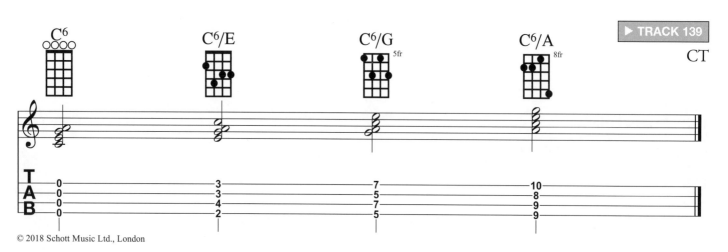

Now in tandem with D6 – leading to a Gma7 – play this **7 7 7 9** if you dont have 14 frets:

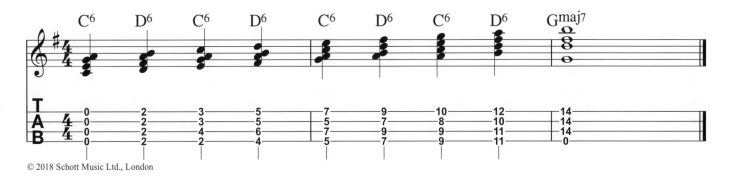

Study 3

A sloping barre – one finger at two different frets – is useful for a diminished chord.
Here it is playing **5 6 5 6** followed by **5 6 5 3** the 1st finger playing 6 on the G string and
then 3 on the A string when the 4th finger is lifted.

Fig. 13

Fig. 14

▶ TRACK 140

CT

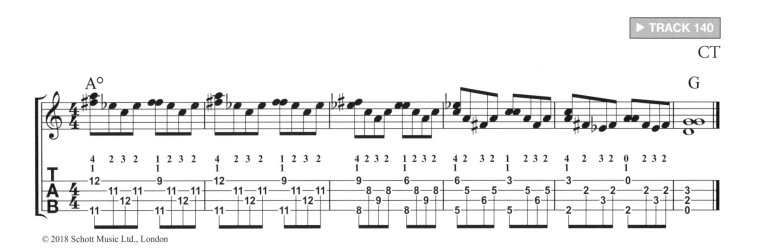

Study 4

Chromatic changes within a chord

▶ TRACK 141

© 2018 Schott Music Ltd., London

Study 5

Barre with different fingers

▶ TRACK 142

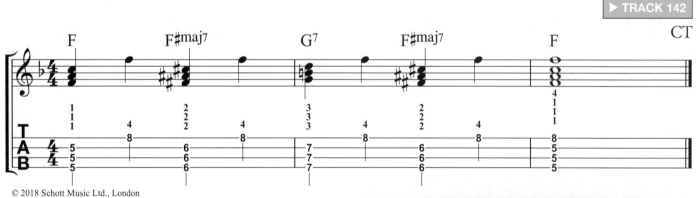

© 2018 Schott Music Ltd., London

This is what F♯ ma7 6 6 6 8 should look like:

Fig. 15

Chapter 17
A practice framework

In sports nowadays players spend a lot of time away from their game by working in the gym or on the track, conditioning muscles and gaining stamina to be ready for the game itself. Many pianists and other instrumentalists spend hours working on scales and exercises to train their fingers to gain strength and flexibility so that, when they tackle the pieces that other people will want to hear, they are prepared.

In this chapter I have put together a set of exercises that will enable ukulele players to have an organised, methodical and easy-to-remember plan to train both hands to have the finger strength, flexibility and agility to play with confidence. In other words, to be physically prepared so that the hands can do what the music demands. The exercises will enable the left hand to become used to the varying distances between frets and to adapt and vary the thumb and wrist position to get a positive contact with the finger tips. The repetition of the right-hand plucking and strumming patterns will also bring its own rewards.

The basic pattern is shown in Study 1 on the A string. I have included note names; learning them will help consolidate your knowledge of the notes on the fretboard. Start by using alternating *i m* in the right hand.

Study 1

▶ TRACK 143

CT

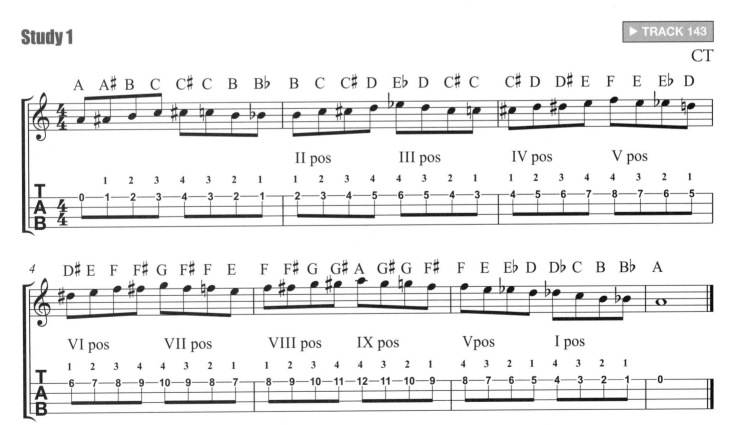

The pattern covers each fret systematically ending with a descending chromatic scale from 12 to Open. Repeat with any other right-hand alternating fingering – *i a, m a, p i, p m, p a.* Try up- and down right-hand strokes with individual fingers, making use of the back of the nail.

Study 1a

Here are the opening measures of the study relocated on other single strings. Use the 7-measure pattern shown in Study 1 each time. Remember after the first measure to move up a fret each time you reach the 4th finger fret and also to change position when you get back to the 1st finger; that way, you will reach the 12th fret with a shift and be ready to start the downward chromatic run.

▶ TRACK 144

CT

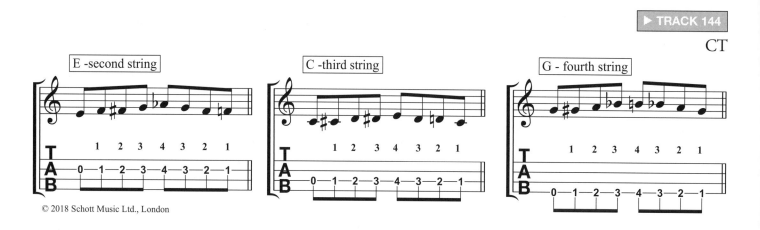

There are many variations of this exercise that you could explore.

Study 2

A jazzy swing time version; it looks exactly the same as Study 1 except for the tempo marking. Listen to the Audio Track to get the feel for it; relaxed and almost lazy, it could even be written in 12/8 time.

▶ TRACK 145

CT

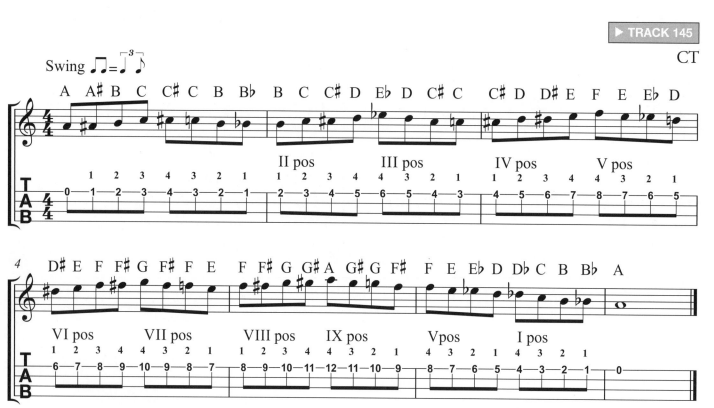

Study 2a

Remember to carry on swinging.

Study 3

Here is the pattern in a more classical rhythm as used in Dvořák's *Humoresque*. The sixteenths are much closer to the following dotted eighths, limping along rather than swinging.

I have left out the full 1st string version as I hope you will have grasped the concept; on the Audio Track I play them in full.

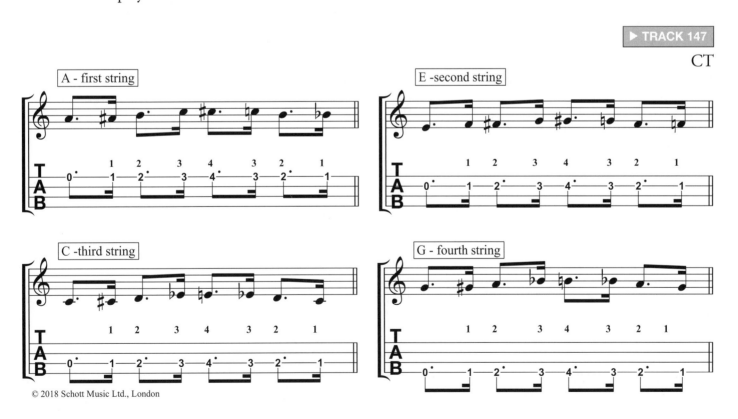

Study 4

Here is **double stopping** within the framework using the A and E strings, showing it in full. It's a good idea to experiment with different LH fingers; here I have shown the most difficult one where you double stop with each finger in turn.

Alternatively, you could try sliding using just one finger or any combination of two fingers. Also try different right-hand patterns, pluck with *i m, p i, m a.* On the C and E strings I like using a down/up brush stroke with *i m*, using the back of the nail for the down strokes. This will prepare you for those rhythmic partial chord sections of a song where you are filling in between the plucked melody notes.

▶ **TRACK 148**

CT

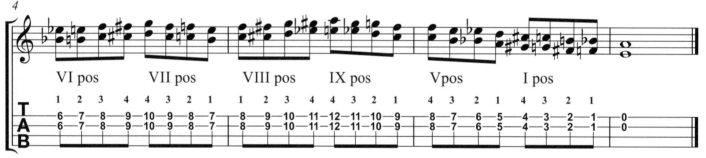

© 2018 Schott Music Ltd., London

Study 4a

The opening measures of double stopping on the other pairs of adjacent strings:

▶ **TRACK 149**

CT

C and E   **G and C**

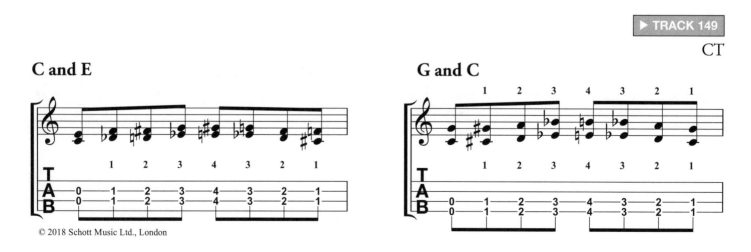

© 2018 Schott Music Ltd., London

Study 5

Triple stopping

Remember: triple stopping on the top three strings produces minor chords, whilst on the bottom three it produces the major versions.

▶ TRACK 150

CT

Study 5a

Now on the lower strings:

▶ TRACK 151

CT

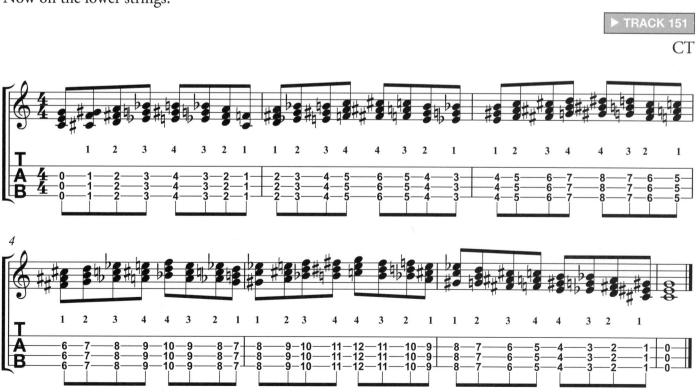

Study 6

Playing this on all four strings is very difficult to do with individual finger barre; try any other fingerings that may be comfortable for you. The chords produced are either minor 7ths (after the note on the A string) or major 6ths (after the note on the C string).

▶ TRACK 152

CT

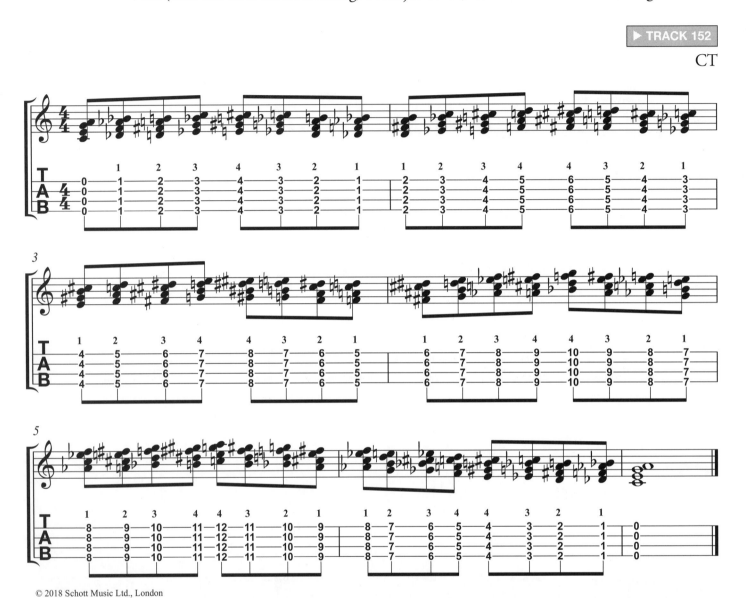

Study 7

Moving up and down through the positions on the neck can be used to practice all other move-able chord shapes. This study starts with the chord of C major. To keep within 12 frets I have changed the model slightly to 6/8 so that the 4-fret stretch still forms a repeatable pattern.

▶ TRACK 153

CT

Study 7a

Starting with F major:

▶ TRACK 154

CT

Study 7b

Starting with A major, it's back to 4/4 for this one with its 5-fret stretch:

Use the framework for any other chords, aiming for accuracy of finger positions and purity of tone rather than speed – that will come over time.

Now go and enjoy your ukulele – anywhere – anytime!

Colin   **Fig. 16**

Appendix 1:
Glossary

Glossary of musical terms used in this book. For further information and definitions consult the many online websites dealing with musical terms and notation.

Accelerando (It.) gradually get faster.

Arpeggio (It. harp style) the notes of a chord played sequentially in a rising or descending order.

Augmented chord (see **chord**)

Barre (Fr. *barré*, barred) the technique whereby a chord is played on the guitar/ukulele by using one or more fingers to press down several strings across a single fret of the fingerboard (like a bar pressing down on the strings). We use the term *bar* as a verb in this book to refer to this instrumental technique.

Blues a musical genre and form originating in the southern states of the USA in the late 19th century. Specifically developed from African-American work songs and spirituals. The 12-BAR BLUES being the most common form.

Cadence the ending of a musical phrase or complete piece. The PERFECT or AUTHENTIC CADENCE ends with the TONIC CHORD (formed on the 1st note of the key scale of the piece) preceded by the DOMINANT CHORD (formed on the 5th note of the key scale):

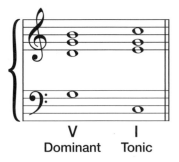

Campanella (It.) sounding in imitation of a little bell. A popular effect in guitar writing.

Chord the simultaneous sounding of two or more pitches or tones. A three-part chord (or triad) can be formed on each note of a major or minor scale by taking that note as its bass and adding the 3rd and 5th notes above it:

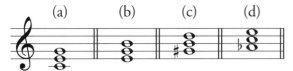

Chord (a) consists of a major 3rd (C–E) plus a perfect 5th (C–G) and is called a MAJOR TRIAD.

Chord (b) consists of a minor 3rd (E–G) plus a perfect 5th (E–B) and is called a MINOR TRIAD.

Chord (c) consists of a minor 3rd (G♯–B) plus a diminished 5th (G♯–D) and is called a DIMINISHED TRIAD.

Chord (d) consists of a major 3rd (A♭–C) plus an augmented 5th (A♭–E) and is called an AUGMENTED TRIAD.

The above triads are said to be in ROOT POSITION as the lowest note (or root) of the basic triad is the bass note. When the root is not in the lowest note in the chord the triad is said to be inverted. Thus there are three positions possible for each triad:

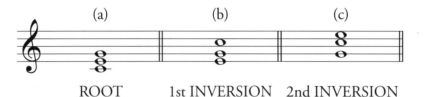

ROOT   1st INVERSION   2nd INVERSION

An ordered series of chords is called a CHORD PROGRESSION such as is found in the 12-bar blues.

Coda (It. tail) a passage that concludes a musical piece or movement often taking the form of an expanded cadence.

Common time refers to music written in 4/4 meter in which a whole note (semibreve) is divided into 4 quarter note beats for each measure (bar). The symbol **C** is sometimes used instead of the numerical sign.

Crescendo (It.) gradually getting louder.

Cut time refers to music written in 2/2 or ₵ meter in which the whole note (semibreve) is divided into 2 half note beats for each measure (bar). It is sometimes referred to as alla breve time.

Da Capo (It. from the beginning) an instruction to play again from the beginning of the piece. The ending is indicated by 'Fine' (end) or by the fermata/pause sign ⌢ or both together.

Diminished chord (see chord)

Dominant (see **chord**)

Drone a note or chord which forms a continuous accompaniment to a melody such as is played on the bagpipes.

Enharmonic two notes which sound exactly the same but are named differently, for example, C sharp and D flat.

Flat the sign ♭ which, when placed before a note on the staff, is an instruction to lower that note by a half tone (semitone).

Grace note a melodic ornament or embellishment usually a short note(s) printed/written in small type and played before the main note(s).

Hammer-on and **Pull-off** related terms (first used and popularized by Pete Seeger) describing specific guitar-playing techniques which can be applied to the ukulele also. A *hammer-on* (the guitarist's equivalent of an ascending slur) describes the action of bringing down the fretting finger ("hammering") onto the fingerboard behind a fret (instead of being plucked or picked in the usual fashion) causing a note to sound. A *pull-off* (the guitarist's equivalent of a descending slur) describes the action of pulling the finger off ("pulling") a string on the fingerboard.

Harmony a combination of musical sounds ordered into a succession of consonant and dissonant chords.

Key signature the group of sharps or flats placed after the clef at the beginning of a piece (and repeated on each subsequent line) to indicate the key.

Legato (It. bound) singing or playing in a smooth, flowing style often notated with a curved slur or phrase mark.

Measure (bar) the vertical lines crossing the staff showing the regular metrical division of the music.

Minor scales in the minor scale some notes may be chromatically altered to emphasize the melodic or harmonic tension. The harmonic minor scale has a raised seventh degree to allow for a convincing dominant-tonic cadence. In the melodic minor scale both the sixth and seventh degrees are raised when ascending, but not when descending.

In A minor:

(a) Harmonic minor:

(b) Melodic minor:

Natural the sign ♮ which, when placed before a note on the staff, is an instruction to cancel an accidental sharp or flat.

Ossia (It. optional) indicates an alternative section or passage, often to show an easier version.

Phrase music may be divided into short units of various lengths similar in structure and function to sentences and phrases in prose writing. Phrasing is often indicated by a long curved line called a slur ⌣ or ⌢ which stretches from the first to the last note of a phrase.

Power chord consists of the root note and the fifth above it (ex. C–G) commonly played on amplified guitars with distortion. Power chords are frequently used in hard rock and heavy metal.

Rasgueado (Sp.) the downward strumming of the strings with the right-hand thumb (or the back of the right-hand fingernails), or an upward sweep over the strings with the fingertips or the thumb.

Repeat signs the instruction to repeat certain musical passages is shown by dots placed within double barlines ‖: :‖; the ending of a repeated passage may be altered on its repetition and this is indicated by the use of 1st and 2nd endings notated thus: ⌐1¬⌐2¬. Other instructions for sectional repeats include the instructions *Da Capo* or *D.C.* meaning 'repeat from the beginning' and *Dal Segno* or *D.S.* meaning 'repeat from the sign' shown as 𝄋. Sometimes the indicated sectional repeat includes the instruction *Da Capo al Fine* or *D.S. al Fine*, which directs the player to repeat the section and to finish at the cadence marked *Fine*.

Round a composition in which each voice (or instrumental part) sings exactly the same melody at the unison but with each voice (or part) beginning at different times in overlap but which fits harmoniously together. Popular and well-known examples include *Three Blind Mice* and *London's Burning* and the French round *Frère Jacques* used in varied guises in this book as *I Love Music*.

Sharp the sign ♯ which, when placed before a note on the staff, is an instruction to raise that note by a half tone (semitone).

Slur a curved line ‿ or ⌒ above or below a group of notes to indicate a phrase.

Swing the term has two main uses (a) a style of jazz originating in the 1930s with an emphasis on solo improvisation (b) a rhythmic style of playing where the pulse is unequally divided usually alternating between long and short durations. For example the first measure of *Blues in C* could be notated and played: ♫ = ⌐3¬♩♪; see also Chapter 17, Study 2.

Syncopation the displacement of the normal accent within a measure normally by a long note placed on a weak beat, for example:

Tied note two notes of the same pitch held as a continuous sound and indicated by a short curved line or tie: ♩‿♩.

Tierce de Picardy (Fr. Picardy third) a tonic major chord played at the end of a piece (or section) set in a minor key.

Time signature figures placed after the clef and key signature at the beginning of a piece. The upper figure indicates the number of beats (units) in each measure, the lower figure the unit of measurement, for example: 3/4 indicates that there are 3 quarter notes (crotchets) in each measure (bar).

Tonic (see **chord**)

Tremolo (It. trembling) a trembling, wavering effect obtained either by (a) moving the finger on a string in a fast but unmeasured rhythm or (b) by a rapid reiteration of a single note with the plucking finger or with a plectrum.

Triad (see **chord**)

Appendix 2:
Fat Fish note names

Try using these note syllables for sharps and flats when singing note names. By adding "ish"
to any sharp note and "at" to any flat the notes can be sung as one syllable sounds.

Here is the chromatic scale from C, ascending using sharps, descending using flats:

Index of tunes

Track listings for downloads

You can download all audio tracks at: en.schott-music.com/fingerstyle-ukulele

Track	Chapter	
1	Ch 1	Tuning GCEA
2		Study 1
3		Study 2
4		**The Westminster Chimes**
5	Ch 2	Study 1
6		Study 2
7		**When the Saints Go Marching In**
8		Study 3
9		**Renaissance Dance**
10	Ch 3	Study 1
11		Study 2
12		**Play Around**
13		Study 3
14		Study 4
15		**Blues in C**
16	Ch 4	Study 1
17		Study 2
18		**Casey Jones**
19		Study 3
20		Study 4
21		**Pay Me My Money Down**
22		Study 5
23		**Lullaby**
24		Study 6
25		**Dziadzia's Tune**
26		**Blues in C with chords**
27		**Wooden Heart**
28	Ch 5	Study 1
29		Study 2
30		**Happy Birthday to You**
31		Study 3
32		**O Tannenbaum**
33		**Mango Walk**

Track	Chapter	
34		Study 4
35		**Deck the Halls**
36		I Love Music (ILM) 1
37		ILM 2
38		ILM 3
39	Ch 6	Study 1
40		Study 2
41		**First Love**
42		Study 3
43		**Swing Low, Sweet Chariot**
44		**Careless Love**
45		**Sloop John B**
46		Study 4
47		**Suo-Gân**
48		ILM 4
49		ILM 5
50	Ch 7	Study 1
51		Study 2
52		Study 3
53		**Song of the Volga Boatmen**
54		Study 4
55		Study 5
56		**The Eagle**
57		ILM 6
58		ILM 7
59	Ch 8	Study 1
60		Study 2
61		Study 3
62		Study 4
63		Study 5
64		Study 6
65		**Malagueña**
66		Study 7
67		Study 8

Track	Chapter	
68		Study 9
69		**Coventry Carol**
70		ILM 8
71		ILM 9
72	Ch 9	Study 1 (a)
73		Study 1 (b)
74		Study 1 (c)
75		Study 2
76		Study 3
77		Study 4 V1
78		Study 4 V2
79		Study 5 V1
80		Study 5 V2
81		**Minuet in D minor**
82		Study 6
83		Study 7
84		**Fürry Reggae**
85		ILM 10
86		ILM 11
87	Ch 10	Study 1
88		Study 2
89		Study 3
90		Study 4
91		**Joshua Fought the Battle of Jericho**
92		Study 5
93		Study 6
94		Study 7
95		Study 7 When The Saints
96		Study 8
97		**Perpetually Diminishing**
98		ILM 12
99		ILM 13
100	Ch 11	Study 1
101		Study 2
102		**Ave Verum Corpus**

Track	Chapter	
103		Study 3
104		Study 4
105		Study 5
106		**La Paloma**
107		ILM 14
108	Ch 12	Study 1
109		Study 2
110		**My Bonnie Lies Over the Ocean**
111		Study 3
112		**All Things Bright and Beautiful**
113		Study 4
114		Study 5
115		**Saltash Blues**
116		ILM 15
117	Ch 13	Study 1
118		Study 2
119		**The Chromatic Rag**
120		**The Strangely-Timed 12-Bar Blues**
121		Study 3
122		Study 4
123		ILM 16
124	Ch 14	Study 1
125		Study 2
126		Study 3
127		Study 4
128		**Romanza**
129		Study 5
130		**Jasmine Flower**
131		Study 6
132		Study 7
133		**Hammer & Pull**
134		ILM 17
135	Ch 15	**All My Trials**
136		**Jupiter**

Track	Chapter	
137		**Swan Lake**
138	Ch 16	Study 1
139		Study 2
140		Study 3
141		Study 4
142		Study 5
143	Ch 17	Study 1
144		Study 1a
145		Study 2
146		Study 2a
147		Study 3
148		Study 4
149		Study 4a
150		Study 5
151		Study 5a
152		Study 6
153		Study 7
154		Study 7a
155		Study 7b

Schott World Music series
for Ukulele

For beginners:

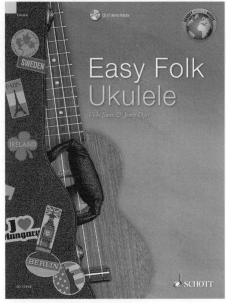

Easy Folk Ukulele

Jonny Dyer & Vicki Swan
36 Traditional Pieces for Ukulele

ED 13848

from Easy Folk Ukulele

from American Folk Tunes for Ukulele

For intermediate to advanced players:

English Folk Tunes for Ukulele
Colin Tribe
37 Traditional Pieces for Ukulele

ED 13569

Irish Folk Tunes for Ukulele
Colin Tribe
36 Traditional Pieces for Ukulele

ED 13577

American Folk Tunes for Ukulele
Colin Tribe
36 Traditional Pieces for Ukulele

ED 13785

SCHOTT
www.schott-music.com